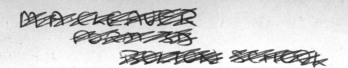

The Young
Air Traveller's
Handbook

A curious mixture of metric and imperial measurements is used in the world of aviation. In this book we have used those measurements which are commonly used by people who work in aviation.

The Young Air Traveller's Handbook

Brian Walters

Hamlyn
London·New York·Sydney·Toronto

Acknowledgements

Illustrations by Derek Bunce, Linden Artists Ltd., Bob Mathias and Michael Turner.

We are grateful to the following for permission to reproduce photographs: ABC Airways Guide 81 top; Aerofilms 68 and 69; Air France 145 insets; Airpix 110, 111 centre and bottom; Debbie Beevor 71; Robin Bernard 9; Boeing Airplane Company 17 top, 41 bottom right; British Aerospace 33 top, 34, 37, 38 and 39, 43, 98, 146, 147; British Airports Authority 21, 46 bottom, 70, 73, 83 bottom, 84 top and bottom, 85 top and bottom, 89 centre left, centre right, bottom right, 92 top, 97, 108, 108 and 109, 112, 126 and 127, 130, 140 and 141 and insets, 203 top, 217 right; British Airways 17 bottom, 19 top and bottom, 23 bottom, 33 centre left and right, 72 top and bottom, 105 inset, 111 top, 138 and 139, 153 top; British Caledonian Airways 4 and 5, 80, 81 bottom, 86, 87, 89 bottom left, 104 and 105, 114 and 115, 116 and 117, 135; Ken Brookes 150 top and bottom; Chubb Fire Security Ltd. 109; R. and J. Coley Ltd, 20; Mary Evans Picture Library 7 bottom, 10 top, 216 left; Flight International 217 left; Tim Howard 176 and 177; Mike Jerram 55 bottom; Laker Airways 79, 119; Lockheed Aircraft Corporation 16, 18 top, 25 top, 203 bottom, 204 and 205, 208 and 209; Lufthansa 82, 100 inset, 104, 106, 131, 133, 151 top and bottom, 153 bottom; Robin Lush 63; Mansell Collection 190; McDonnel Douglas Corporation 1, 2 and 3, 18 bottom, 23 top, 24, 28 bottom, 41 top, centre and bottom left, 122 and 123, 132, 206; Metropolitan Police 107; NASA 210 and 211; Radio Times Hulton Picture Library 191 top and bottom; RFD-GQ Ltd. 99, 137; Royal Aircraft Establishment 33 bottom; Short Brothers Ltd. 28 centre; Adrian South 57 top, 58; Tilbury Files 7 top, 8, 25 bottom, 29, 46 top, 55 top, 62, 88, 100 and 101, 118, 121, 145, 156 and 157, 196 and 197, 200 and 201, 200 inset, 207 top, 216 right; Vought Corporation 83 top, 90 and 91, 113 top and bottom; Harry Watts 6.

Jacket photographs: British Airports Authority main picture; Lufthansa front insets; Tilbury file back left inset; British Caledonian back right inset.

Contents

This page The DC-10 BRITISH CALEDONIAN has been used by many airlines to replace the Boeing 707.

Previous page Company demonstrators such as this DC-10 helped to win orders from many airlines.

Air transport~a success story of the 20th century

For thousands of years man has envied the birds their ability to soar effortlessly about the sky.

Little is known of the earliest attempts to get airborne and it is unlikely that we will ever be certain if the Chinese were, in fact, the first to practise the art of lifting a man into the sky – on a kite. Or perhaps an earlier civilisation in Peru had produced a device to carry men aloft? Gigantic figures carved on a plain in Peru could surely have only been planned by someone who could reach a height of several hundred feet above the ground – at least, this is the belief held by some present-day experts who have tested the theory by producing a hot-air balloon from natural materials available in the country.

In Egypt a wooden model of a bird discovered in Saqqara looks not unlike a glider. Maybe it is simply a poor reproduction of a bird – or maybe it is a hint that as long ago as 400 B.C. man had conquered the air.

Right Sir George Cayley is regarded as the 'father' of aviation. His experiments did much to advance the theories of flight.

Top Man has long been unwilling to concede the fact that birds are better designed to fly than we are. However after years of vain effort man-powered flight has made great advances with the Gossamer Condor and Gossamer Albatross craft designed by Paul MacCready.

Left Fine light-weight bones and millions of years of evolution make the birds the most efficient flying creatures.

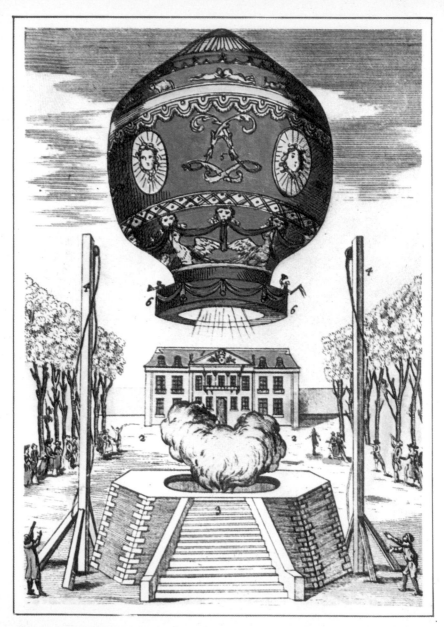

Be that as it may, it was not until 1903 that the era of the aeroplane was opened. Far-seeing scientists and inventors like Leonardo da Vinci in the fifteenth century and George Cayley, three centuries later, had produced plans which we can recognise today as being not unlike early successful aircraft. For years, however, the supporters of lighter-than-air craft could point to the success of the Montgolfier brothers who built many man-carrying hot air balloons. As a means of transport, however, a balloon is subject to the vagaries of the wind. It has therefore never progressed beyond being a pleasurable means of floating over the countryside and even today – some 200 years later – the sport of hot air ballooning continues to thrive. French inventive-

Left The Montgolfier brothers in 1783 succeeded in an experiment with a hot air balloon.

Below Today, many hot air balloons are sponsored by companies such as Beaver Books.

ness developed the balloon into an airship, by changing the shape of the 'envelope' and suspending a gondola beneath it. Powered by a steam engine, the strange craft introduced powered flight for the first time. But it is the name of Count Ferdinand von Zeppelin which will always be linked with the airship. His enthusiasm for this form of transport led to the first regular air services between several German cities in 1910 and later to the gigantic *Graf Zeppelin* and *Hindenberg* airships. These majestic craft carried thousands of passengers in comfort and safety until several disasters in the 1930s.

Top Astonishingly, 61 people survived the Hindenberg disaster in 1937.

Although several brave pioneers had learned how to control gliders, the development of heavier-than-air craft had to await the internal combustion engine before aircraft could take off under their own power.

Thousands of passengers were carried safely on board the giant Zeppelins. Comfortable and spacious, they were truly the 'ships of the air'.

The Wright brothers
and their *Flyer*.

The young Wright brothers did not realise it at the time, but their short powered hop in the *Flyer* was to open the floodgates to further rapid development in aviation. The spur to such development, however, was to be provided by the First World War. The performance and efficiency of the aeroplane improved enormously during this terrible conflict and the influence on air transport was soon to be made clear. Hundreds of young pilots survived the war with a firm ambition to remain in aviation. Military aircraft, too, were available in abundance and many were converted to carry passengers. Thus was the infant airline industry born from the ashes of war. Europe had the aircraft, the pilots and the urgent need for a transport system to supplement the war-torn rail and road system. America, on the other hand, had an excellent railway system and a less urgent need to develop airlines. Each European country had different motives in building up an airline. Imperial nations such as France, Belgium and Great Britain were principally concerned with forging air links with their empires in different parts of the world. Germany, however, had a driving ambition to extend her influence throughout the world, and as a consequence gradually became a leading power in aviation.

The sudden flowering of airlines after the First World War soon gave way to a period of confusion. The converted bombers proved to be expensive to operate and resulted in many airlines falling by the wayside. Those that did survive demanded new and more efficient airliners. Firms like Junkers and Fokker rose to the challenge and produced aircraft which were the first airliners to be produced in substantial numbers. The Junkers F.13 of the 1920s, for example, saw service with airlines all over the world; fitted with wheels, floats or skis, this four-seat airliner was the foundation upon which many airlines were built.

Anthony Fokker's F.2 of the same period was also only a four-seater but was later followed by larger and equally successful designs.

For a period before the Second World War, the flying boat gained a supremacy over other types of airliner. Its chief advantage was that it could fly to parts of the world where there were no runways but, although comfortable and regarded with affection by passengers, it was both slow and unprofitable. Just before the outbreak of war in 1939 a Focke-Wulf Condor flew non-stop from Berlin to New York. The flight took over 24 hours but it opened the era of the long-distance land-plane.

The Fokker tri-plane and the SE5 (*left*) gained fame during the First World War. By the 1930s Shorts had produced their famous range of flying boats (*inset*).

In America, airlines were slow to come into existence. Airmail services flown by retired military aircraft mushroomed after the First World War but most of the budding airlines were too small and weak financially to be able to survive. In the 1930s an element of political sharp practice was used to help the formation of larger and stronger airlines. However, these strong airlines were instrumental in helping to establish a thriving aircraft industry in the United States – an industry which grew to dominate the world. Boeing, Douglas and Lockheed produced airliners which began to challenge the leading aircraft industries of Germany, France, Italy and Britain.

The DC-3 of the late 1930s was the first really profitable and successful airliner. A revolutionary aircraft for its day, it has since become a classic design which remains in service over forty years later. Of 11,000 built, some 1,000 DC-3s are still flying today – a truly remarkable record. With one bound, America had, in the DC-3, leapt ahead of Europe which was still using such slow and ungainly aircraft as the German Junkers Ju 52/3m and the British Handley-Page HP 42.

Once again it took a war to bring about the next resurgence in air travel; the Second World War accelerated the development of aircraft which were to influence the course of the conflict. Just as in the First World War, new production methods were devised and the performance of aircraft greatly improved. Of course, these improvements to fighters and bombers became available to airliners after the war and new air services soon got under way when the battlefields were hushed.

Trans-Atlantic services, which had so taxed pioneering airlines before the war, became commonplace as aircraft with sufficient

During the Second World War rocket-and cannon-armed Typhoons supported the invasion forces in Normandy, while the Dakota was an invaluable transport.

range became available. Transport aircraft such as the DC-4 and Constellation were the means by which regular services over the ocean were inaugurated, although their limited range obliged stops in both Ireland and Newfoundland.

The post-war desire to travel and to see foreign lands created a growing demand for air services. The need to rebuild countries shattered by war also stimulated the establishment of air links.

Britain did not repeat its earlier neglect of European air services which left it far behind the leaders in air transport. A network was quickly established by BEA, while BOAC looked after the longer routes. The two airlines soon grew to become major carriers and have merged to form British Airways.

Competition between airlines and a steady growth in traffic led to the development of bigger and better airliners culminating in the Douglas DC-7C and the Lockheed Super-Constellation. Pressurised cabins had made long journeys more comfortable as the airliners could climb to greater heights enabling them to leave rough weather far below. These aircraft were the ultimate in piston-engined airliner development, being capable of flying great distances, including across the Atlantic, non-stop. Their days, however, were numbered. Even before the end of the war, a committee of experts in Britain was planning the introduction of some revolutionary airliners. The jet engine which had completely changed military aviation was to be given a civil application. In 1952 BOAC introduced the 36-seat de Havilland Comet I into service. It was the first faltering step into the jet age. Alas, two Comets later crashed into the Mediterranean in mysterious circumstances and it was only after a difficult salvage operation followed by a minute inspection of the wreckage that metal fatigue was established as the cause. There could be no question of commercial secrecy in such a vital matter as air safety and the results of the investigation into the cause of the Comet crashes were circulated to leading manufacturers worldwide.

Another promising British design which failed to match up to its early promise was the Bristol Britannia. A four turbo-prop powered airliner, the Britannia could have taken business from Lockheed and Douglas had it not suffered long production delays.

The Lockheed Super Constellation represented the ultimate in piston-engined airliner design.

The turbo-fan powered Boeing 707 *(top)* proved to be one of the most efficient airliners of the first 'jet generation'. The Bristol Britannia *(above)* was the bridge between the piston-engined and jet eras.

With the Vickers Viscount Britain had an unqualified success. Turbo-prop power brought new standards of comfort and speed, ensuring that the type sold well in most parts of the world including the United States. The gas turbine revolution caught some manufacturers unawares, however; Lockheed and Douglas had been the main suppliers of long-distance airliners since the war but were ill-prepared to produce jet airliners. Boeing, on the other hand, had amassed valuable experience in building large jet bombers and it was not difficult to draw on that experience when it came to building a jet airliner. In the Boeing 707, the company produced an airliner which quickly gained orders from many airlines anxious to remain competitive. Douglas responded with the DC-8 and it, too, found customers, particularly among airlines which had bought its designs since the days of the DC-3. Lockheed did not even enter the 'jet race', choosing instead to produce the Electra, a turbo-prop airliner.

Top Lockheed's turbo-prop powered Electra. *Above* An unusually decorated DC-8.

Similar in size to the Electra, the Vickers Vanguard did not enjoy the world-wide sales of the earlier Viscount and it may be argued that BEA did not appreciate the speed of the jet revolution in short-haul services. Only in Russia did a large four turbo-prop airliner achieve substantial sales; the IL-18 was widely used by the East European airlines and some were operated by 'third world' countries.

A re-engined and strengthened Comet was produced and gave good service to airlines which did not need aircraft as large as the Boeing 707 or the DC-8. Almost overnight aircraft such as Lockheed's L.1649A Super Starliner became outdated. Airliners which had proudly carried the flags of leading carriers all over the world were retired altogether or purchased by charter airlines which were not then concerned with the 'jet race'.

Britain's answer to the Boeing 707 and the DC-8 was the Vickers VC-10, a very elegant aircraft which, unfortunately, was less economical than its American rivals. It was to be Britain's last attempt to compete in this class of airliner.

Mention must be made of Russia's contribution to the jet age. Preferring to remain aloof from the Western world, Russia has never played a major role in world commercial aviation. Her territory and that of the other Eastern bloc countries covers a very large geographical area and the Soviet airline Aeroflot, the largest airline in the world, has been chiefly concerned to maintain links within this area. As a consequence the rest of the world was largely unaware that following the withdrawal of the Comet services the Russian Tu-104 was the only jet airliner in regular service from 1956 until the commencement of Comet 4 and Boeing 707 services in 1958.

The Comet 4 was the successor to the ill-fated Comet 1.
The Vickers Vanguard ended its days with British Airways as a freighter.

The capacity of the new jets was considerably greater than that of the aircraft which they replaced. The early Boeing 707 had about double the payload of the Super-Constellation, for example.

With all the leading airlines equipping themselves with jets, there simply were not enough passengers to fill them. Slowly, however, traffic grew to match the capacity offered by the airlines and the early massive losses were turned into handsome profits. After initial teething troubles, the jets proved to be far more reliable than the piston-engined airliners. For although powerful motors had been developed for the DC-7 and Super-Constellation, they were both complicated and difficult to maintain. With fewer moving parts and a far lower level of vibration, the jet engine was a welcome step forward for airlines.

A sad end for the flying-boat.

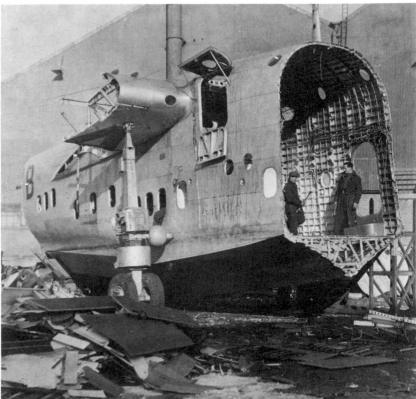

Thanks to the 'jumbos' it is commonplace for passengers to visit Australia.

It was not long before jet airliners ousted piston-engined aircraft from shorter routes too. The piston-engined Convair 440 had managed to hold its own against the turbo-prop Viscount – they both had propellers after all – but the arrival of the Caravelle upon the scene began another revolution. This time the Super-Constellations which had managed to find a job carrying passengers over short distances really had to retire. For most it was to the breaker's yard, for a few a place in a museum or perhaps as a roadside café ensured that they were not entirely forgotten.

It is a proven fact that speed generates traffic. The ability to fly to and from a city in one day led businessmen to leave their offices more often in pursuit of trade. Air travel became the accepted means for thousands who had previously never considered flying. The 'package' holiday was, for an increasing number of people, a simple and inexpensive way to enjoy the Mediterranean sun.

In the United States only the motor car could resist the relentless growth of air services. The railway system was the first to succumb and the airlines have long since become the principal means of public transport between the cities. The networks of the airlines grew to encompass every city.

21

Some European aircraft manufacturers, conceding that they could not build large airliners to compete with the Americans, turned to the task of building a DC-3 replacement. In 1955 Fokker flew the F-27 Friendship for the first time and for over 20 years the type has remained in production but although the F-27 made its mark as a tough little airliner, the DC-3 has soldiered on. The Avro 748 and Handley-Page Herald followed Fokker's lead, the former achieving some success in various parts of the world, but the DC-3 just was not willing to be put out to grass.

As new aircraft at the lower end of the scale were introducing air transport to smaller communities, constant improvements were made to the big jets. Improved engines and lengthened fuselages resulted in the most economical airliners which the carriers had yet operated. Able to maintain or even lower fares, the airlines attracted more and more passengers; the late 1960s were boom years in which an increasing number of passengers meant healthy balance sheets.

Improvements to long-haul aircraft were matched by the introduction of new equipment on medium and short-haul routes. De Havilland designed the Trident to meet BEA's requirements for the 1960s and various marks of the aircraft saw service in the ensuing years. The Boeing 727 was, like the Trident, powered by three engines and

indeed it did not appear until after the British design, but it has become the most successful jet airliner ever built. The Boeing 727 was both popular with passengers and a money-maker – small wonder that orders have topped 1600 and are still growing!

The twin-engined BAC One-Eleven was also ahead of its rival the Douglas DC-9 but once again the American design far outsold the British aircraft. It must be said that the giant American domestic carriers provide the sort of market which must be the envy of all manufacturers. This very strong home market is one reason why United States manufacturers supply no less than 80% of the world's airline markets.

It is clear that many significant advances in air transport have been due to military pressure, however indirect. The next step forward in air transport was also to be the result of a military requirement. The United States Air Force need for a giant transport aircraft led to design submissions from several companies. In the event, Lockheed won the contract and the C-5A Galaxy is the result. Boeing, however, decided to develop its own design and offered it to Pan American Airways. Once again the American airline led the way with an order for a fleet of Boeing 747s. The sudden growth of a decade earlier was repeated as the major airlines of the world queued to buy

Above The DC-9 Series Ten could carry about 70 passengers.
Below Modern construction techniques were used to produce the Trident.

the 300-tonne giant. As before, the capacity of the new 360-seat airliner was a massive increase over earlier equipment. History did not repeat itself precisely, however, for the earlier jets remained in service and were not immediately supplanted by the 747. The popularity of wide-bodied aircraft soon resulted in more designs in this class. The DC-10 and TriStar competed for orders from airlines which did not require the capacity of Boeing's giant. At the lower end of the scale, Europe's 240-seat Airbus provided a serious challenge to American manufacturers for the first time since the Viscount and BAC 1-11 sold in the United States.

Despite the increased costs imposed by the rise in fuel prices, the 'wide-bodies' were a major advance. Once more lower fares boosted passenger loads and despite a world trade recession the 1970s saw a further boom in business.

There can surely be no other industry which matches the growth of the airlines. The fact that a slow uncomfortable flight across the Atlantic cost £110 in 1948 but only £59 for the same journey in jet comfort 30 years later is surely proof of a unique success. The astonishing speed of the Anglo-French Concorde has tended to be overshadowed by the rise of low-cost long distance travel.

Although the DC-10 is designed with many access doors, passenger boarding of such wide-bodied airliners is usually limited to two.

Above The TriStar — Lockheed's wide-bodied airliner.
Below The Boeing 747 remains unchallenged as the largest airliner in the world.

How an aircraft is built

An airliner weighing over 300 tonnes able to sail majestically through the air is, for some, little short of a miracle.

For it is only just over 75 years ago that the Wright brothers finally found the right formula to open the era of powered flight. Then, as now, designers had to produce a structure which combined strength with lightness. It has remained a constant struggle to improve the efficiency of aircraft by reducing weight without compromising safety.

Although the early frail bi-planes are mere museum-pieces today, some of the first construction principles have remained unaltered. Bamboo, fabric, wood and wire, such as were used by the pioneers of aviation, have been superseded by aluminium, steel and plastic but the basic components used today are remarkably similar to those fashioned in the first aircraft factories.

Designers learned that nature provides many examples of strength and lightness; the strength of the tubular shape of bamboo, for example, has led to the use of steel and aluminium tube, and ribs originally

Replicas of some early aircraft have been built for films and may be seen flying at air displays.

fashioned in spruce for a combination of flexibility and strength have given way to metal.

The early aircraft derived strength and lightness from a fabric-covered 'skeleton' and the first major advance in the technique of aircraft construction utilised the *monocoque* method: a strong shell of laminated wood replaced the skeleton of the fuselage, the shell itself taking some of the structural load. The sheets of wood eventually gave way to metal, although wood was still widely used until the late 1930s. The first all-metal airliner was produced in Germany by Professor Junkers as early as 1919. Its strong cantilever wing did away with the need for supporting struts or bracing wires; a beam running the length of the wing provided the necessary strength and the cantilever construction method ultimately became the standard for most airliners. In 1929 another German, Adolf Rohbach, devised the stressed skin method of wing construction. Relatively large panels of sheet metal were riveted to the ribs and spars, bearing some of the stresses previously borne by the aircraft's 'skeleton', thus extending the monocoque principle to the wings. As fewer components are necessary using the stressed skin method, considerable savings in weight are achieved and the performance of the aeroplane is improved.

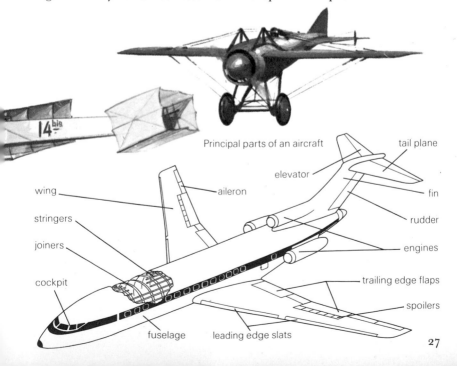

Principal parts of an aircraft

tail plane

wing

aileron

elevator

fin

stringers

rudder

joiners

engines

cockpit

trailing edge flaps

spoilers

fuselage

leading edge slats

The first aircraft production lines were established not in the United States but in Britain. A factory established by the brothers Oswald, Horace and Eustace Short in 1909 manufactured six Flyers for the Wright brothers. Each aircraft was made up of 3,000 separate parts, all of which were produced before assembly of the six aircraft began.

The First World War provided an opportunity to develop production-line techniques. Furniture manufacturers were pressed into service to produce hundreds of aircraft for the fighting services. After the war some time elapsed before the demand for airliners resulted in

Above The Short brothers. *Below* Donald W. Douglas. Here he is seen holding a model of the DC-8 – the first jet airliner produced by his company.

new production-lines being established. Apart from the Junkers F.13 and a series of Fokker designs, few airliners were produced in large quantities. Not, that is, until the 1930s when Donald Douglas produced the DC-3, now regarded as the first modern airliner. Clearly the forerunner of the present-day airliner, the DC-3 was manufactured in thousands. Once again the demands of war led to further refinements in production-line techniques so that military demands could be met. The DC-3 was one of the first production airliners to incorporate a fully retractable undercarriage, along with an all-metal monoplane construction. They also were the first to use a 'fail safe' multi-spar wing – should one spar fail another could bear the load.

Airliners have evolved into many different types and shapes but the process of producing each one has remained much the same. The shape of the airliner is determined by the task which it has to perform. To see if the planned shape is the most efficient possible, scale models are made and tested in a wind tunnel.

This method of investigation was first used in the 1880s by Horatio Phillips, an English aviation pioneer who measured the lift and drag forces of a series of airfoils. The Wright brothers, too, built their own wind tunnel to prove their theories. The similarity in appearance of the Boeing 707 and the DC-8, the BAC One-Eleven and the DC-9, etc. testify to the basic correctness of these designs. Produced to undertake similar tasks, the shapes of these airliners were almost bound to resemble each other!

Accurately made models and wind tunnels play an important part in the design of aircraft. Here a Westland helicopter design is prepared for a test.

A model of the DC-10 is installed in a wind tunnel to see if the designer's theories are correct. Many changes to the design may be made before construction of a prototype is started.

Technicians can view the airflow in the wind tunnel by watching the movement of smoke or tufts of wool fixed to the model. It may be necessary to produce several variations of a basic aircraft design before a decision can be taken to produce an airliner. Compromises have to be made; a higher speed may have to be sacrificed for additional range by extending the wings a little. A bigger fuselage will accommodate bulky loads but will produce more drag and increase weight. Aero-dynamicists aided by computers can accurately calculate the performance of the new design. The shape and area of the wing, the engine power necessary to achieve the required performance and the amount of lifting capacity – the payload – can all be estimated by skilled aerodynamicists.

Stressmen next take a hand by calculating the loads which the various parts of the aircraft will have to bear. The size of such components as the wing spars and the thickness of the skin are carefully estimated.

With their task complete, the stressmen pass their calculations to weight engineers who examine the proposed structure and calculate the total weight of the airliner. At this stage it is possible to determine if the original weight projections are going to be met. Remember the task of a design team is to produce an aircraft that can perform well and carry a profitable load. Many aircraft designs have been failures because they could not carry an adequate number of passengers or enough fuel.

At this stage in the process of producing an airliner hundreds of highly-trained people carry the project a stage further. Thousands of drawings are prepared so that the structure can be built by skilled engineers. Experts in hydraulic systems design a layout for the new airliner and yet more drawings are produced. The same process is applied to the electrical and control circuits and the project now involves many companies in addition to the aircraft manufacturer. Components are selected on the basis of safety, efficiency and cost; hydraulic jacks, the undercarriage, generators, navigation equipment, cables – the 'shopping list' seems endless.

Many thousands of hours have to be spent and hundreds of drawings have to be produced before an airliner begins to take shape.

The task of the stressmen is by no means over, however, for the spectre of a metal fatigue disaster cannot be far from a designer's mind. The spectacular crashes of the Comet I in the 1950s highlighted the dangers of metal fatigue. An airliner's fuselage is subjected to repeated cycles of expansion and contraction as the aircraft climbs to high altitudes. As it reaches 35,000ft the cabin pressure will remain at about 7,000ft so that the passengers may travel in comfort without the need for oxygen masks.

Other stresses are imposed upon the aircraft; turbulence may cause the fuselage to twist, the wings to flex and the tail to shake. The stressmen must be sure each component can withstand far more than the expected loads.

The phenomenon of metal fatigue has been known for some time and a Junkers F.13 was the first aircraft to be subjected to the Royal Aircraft Establishment's painstaking investigation after one broke up in the air. The wreckage of the F.13 was taken to Farnborough and, as far as possible, rebuilt. This technique helps to point to the cause of a failure and skilled technicians can discover the sequence of an accident. In the case of the Comet I, wreckage was dredged up from the sea bed and taken to Farnborough where metal fatigue was conclusively proved to be the culprit.

One consequence of this unhappy chapter in aviation history is that present-day airliners undergo exhaustive tests before they are licensed to carry passengers. Complete aeroplanes are built but never fly. Instead they are subjected to stresses far exceeding those expected in normal operation. The fuselage endures repeated cycles which represent more than the planned lifetime of the aircraft; years of flight can be simulated in a few months. The wings and tail too are attached to jacks which set up vibrations or even severe flexing to determine the ultimate strength of the components. To ensure that the cockpit windows can sustain a strike from a large bird – the known cause of several accidents – a compressed air gun is used to fire a 2kg chicken carcase at speeds of up to 400 knots.

As well as the static test rig, two other non-flying examples of a new airliner are built; a wooden mock-up and an 'iron bird'. The mock-up is a useful method of showing potential customers what the new aircraft will look like and, at the same time, various interior layouts can be tried out. The flight deck is particularly important and is carefully reproduced so that pilots can comment on the visibility and the position of the controls. The 'iron bird' or systems mock-up is a 'real' aeroplane without its skin. Miles of cables, pipes and linkages are installed to ensure that the planned design works in practice. Any difficulties can be ironed out before production gets under way.

The de Havilland Comet (*top*) heralded the jet age in air transport (*above*). But the tragic crashes of the early 1950s (*below*) taught the risks of metal fatigue.

The cockpits of tomorrow will look something like this simplified layout. Cathode ray tube displays replace the dials which are a feature of present-day panels.

As draughtsmen get to work producing thousands of detailed drawings, plans are made for the production of the aircraft. Many different types of alloy are ordered for parts of the aircraft, each having a particular quality of strength, resistance to heat or ability to withstand repeated flexing. Small components are obtained from subcontractors and the layout of the production line is planned for the assembly area.

The positions of jigs and machine tools are carefully considered so that as components and materials are fed into the line the aircraft will gradually take shape and proceed smoothly towards the factory door and the flight line beyond.

Parts of the aircraft, such as skin panels, are produced on wooden formers over which aluminium sheet is stretched so that it takes on the required shape. The sheet is gripped by jaws attached to hydraulic jacks which then pull the panel over the wooden former. Most large panels are produced in this way. Other components are stamped by powerful presses; some large parts which are called upon to bear heavy loads may be made from forgings which are squeezed or hammered into shape, then machined to the correct dimensions.

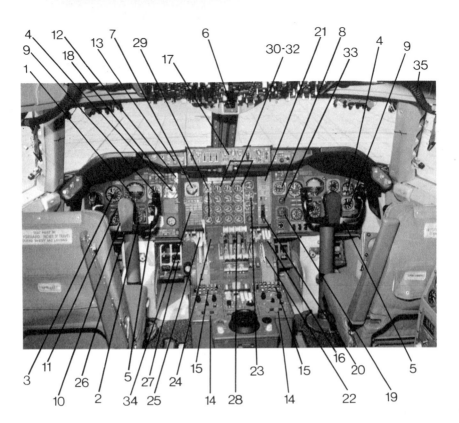

(1) director horizon
(2) flight compass
(3) airspeed indicator
(4) altimeter
(5) vertical speed indicator
(6) magnetic compass
(7) standby horizon
(8) standby altimeter
(9) radio altimeters
(10) radio magnetic indicator
(11) distance measuring equipment (DME)
(12) marker lights
(13) VHF navigation frequency
(14) VHF communications frequency selector
(15) radio selector box
(16) inertial navigation system (INS)
(17) autopilot (a/p)
(18) a/p and flight director mode indicators
(19) a/p trim indicators
(20) undercarriage selector
(21) undercarriage lights
(22) flap selector
(23) flap position indicator
(24) airbrake selector
(25) stabilator trim
(26) flying controls
(27) rudder pedals
(28) throttles
(29) engine instruments number one engine
(30–32) engine instruments numbers 2–4 engines
(33) outside air temperature
(34) central warning system
(35) smoke and oxygen masks

Wing spars, undercarriage struts and engine mountings are produced from forgings. Sometimes if a key part has to bear great stresses it is produced in steel instead of aluminium alloy. Titanium is often used in parts of an airliner's structure, particularly in 'hot' areas which are subject to particular stress. The exhaust and other hot parts of the engine obviously tax the skill of the design team which must ensure that the correct materials are used to make the aeroplane safe. Honeycomb panels are used extensively in airliner construction. Made from a sandwich of aluminium sheet and honeycomb cells of the same material it combines strength with lightness. Having noise absorption qualities, honeycomb panels are often incorporated into engine pods where they play a part in reducing the jet whine.

Various methods are used to attach the fuselage skin to the stringers and to the frames which strengthen the structure. The earliest method and one which is still in use today is by riveting. Although a relatively simple method of attaching one piece of metal to another, it does involve drilling holes, thus creating a potential source of weakness. The muted scream of compressed air drills followed by the rivet guns echoes around the factory as the components take shape. Although hand riveting is still carried out in many factories, giant computer-controlled machines automatically carry out the drilling, reaming, riveting and milling processes in some modern plants.

There is another method of mating skins to stringers – that of gluing or bonding. This has the advantage of avoiding holes, inevitable in

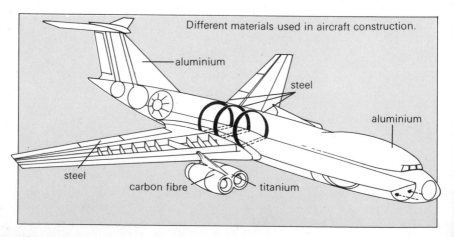

Different materials used in aircraft construction.

aluminium

steel

aluminium

steel

carbon fibre

titanium

Carefully made jigs provide 'patterns' which enable components to be built with great accuracy. Here parts of the One-Eleven airliner are being built in Romania.

riveted joins, but the process is more complex. It involves applying a synthetic resin glue to both metal surfaces and then joining them together under pressure and heat in an 'autoclave' – a type of pressure-oven. Although perhaps more difficult than riveting, bonded parts are joined together along a continuous area whereas riveted sections are only joined where there are holes.

An increasing number of aircraft components are milled from large solid alloy billets, some as long as 13 metres or more. Such is the complexity of modern aircraft design that the thickness of the skin varies from place to place as dictated by the strength requirements.

In areas of greatest stress such as a cut-out for a window or an access panel it is necessary to have a relatively thick skin, whilst neighbouring areas can safely be much thinner. The use of giant numerically-controlled milling machines results in a very strong and accurately produced component. The desired shape is recorded on a magnetic tape which precisely controls the movement of the cutting heads. Quite complex shapes can be produced in this way, sometimes involving as much as 90% of the billet being drilled away. Large containers on the shop floor are frequently filled with 'swarf', metal shavings cut away by the drills.

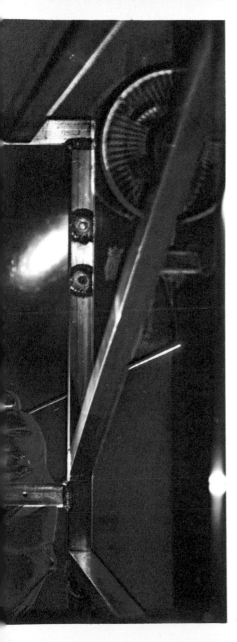

Chemical milling is another process in widespread use today in the production of skins and other components. Thin and thick areas on a skin section are carefully marked, the thick areas being masked by a special protective coating. The part is then placed into an acid bath for a specified time. When it is taken out the skin is of the graduated thickness required by the designers. It is not possible to produce very complex shapes by chemical milling but electro-chemical machining is a development of the 'bath' process which does permit more complicated work. Immersed in a bath of salty electrolyte, the metal is 'cut' by a powerful electric current beamed from a copper tool. Understandably, masks must be worn by those who work in the bath areas as the fumes are unpleasant.

Each of these methods which involve cutting from the solid results in an 'integral' structure; that is one in which there are no joins which may be a potential point of metal fatigue. The components are inherently stronger than fabricated parts and far more resistant to metal fatigue.

Some aircraft parts are welded together to achieve a perfect bond, electron beam and laser techniques being used to ensure great accuracy and consistent results. Electron

Because of their location some components have to be welded by hand. Others can be joined together by huge automatic welding machines.

beam welding is widely used on components where normal methods would be impossible because of difficulty of access.

Jigs or frames of many sizes are built so that the series of components are made to the same precise patterns. Some jigs are very large, being concreted to the factory floor to take such components as the wing. The mating of the wing and fuselage takes place in another jig and at this stage the airliner begins to assume a recognisable shape. As more and more pieces are added to the growing airliner the need for accuracy becomes clear. Thousands of parts built to very exact measurements are brought together like pieces of a jig-saw puzzle. Throughout the whole manufacturing process accuracy is the watchword. 'Make-do' will *not* do when it comes to making aeroplanes, and at every stage of construction, inspectors check the components to make sure that sizes are correct.

When the shell of the aircraft has been completed, there remains much to do. Miles of cables, control runs, hydraulic pipes, and the fuel and oxygen systems must be installed. These and many more items which go to make up an airliner are installed by fitters and electricians. The 'iron bird' has played its part so the intricate web of controls and equipment fits accurately into its allotted space. As the flying controls, engines, undercarriage, etc. are controlled from the flight deck,

it is the scene of feverish activity. There is little room to spare on a flight deck for the technicians as they install and test each connection.

Even when the completed airliner is wheeled out resplendent in its new paint, more tests have to be carried out before it can be flown. When all is ready, the aircraft is test-flown and necessary adjustments made before it is handed over to an airline to begin its career.

Just as wood gave way to metal, so plastic in one form or another seems destined to become the material of the future. Fibreglass has long been used for 'secondary structures' – that is to say, non-load-bearing parts of the aircraft. Many helicopter blades are made of glass fibre now that cheaper methods of production have been devised. Machines have been developed to lay glass fibre tapes ready for impregnation with resins. Subsequently the rotor-blade is put through another process which involves heat and high pressure. The finished product is stronger, lighter and more reliable than metal rotor blades.

Carbon fibre materials have been incorporated in aircraft structures for some time. Stronger and lighter than metal, these 'plastic composites' must be thoroughly tested before they are used to build a wing or a fuselage. Nevertheless it seems likely that towards the end of this century 'plastic' airliners will become commonplace.

Stages in manufacturing an aircraft: *top* DC9s; *centre* and *bottom left* DC10s; *bottom right* completed 747

The wonder of flight

Be it applied to a giant Jumbo or to a small air taxi craft, the principle of flight remains the same. A carefully shaped wing pulled or pushed at speed through the air will provide lift.

To understand just why a fast-moving wing will rise from the ground it must be remembered that air has weight and is fluid. A close look at the wing on an aircraft will reveal that it is curved more on the upper surface than the lower. This is because when air (or any fluid substance) flows over a curved surface not only does it flow faster but this increase in speed is accompanied by a decrease in pressure. Thus as air flows more rapidly over the curved upper surface of the wing, the pressure drops so that lift naturally follows.

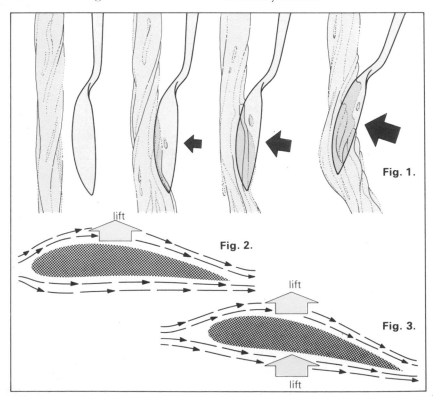

Fig. 1.

lift

Fig. 2.

lift

Fig. 3.

lift

A training aircraft has to be very strong to withstand aerobatic flight.

A simple experiment with a spoon in flowing water will illustrate the effect of a fluid substance on a curved surface (figure 1). As the curved surface of a lightly-held spoon comes into contact with water pouring from a tap, the change in pressure draws the spoon into the flow. It might be thought that the flowing water would push the spoon away but its 'aerofoil' shape acts just like a wing – you will see that it 'rises' into the water.

The aerofoil in figure 2 more closely resembles a typical wing although, as we shall see, the shape of a wing can be altered in various ways. What is called the 'angle of attack' (the angle at which the wing strikes the air through which it is travelling) has a further effect on the ability of the wing to provide lift. Figure 3 shows how, by slightly tilting the wing relative to the flow

of air, some lift can be derived from the under-surface of the wing too. This results in about two-thirds of the lift being provided by the upper surface of the wing and one-third from below. Although the pressure varies over the surface of the wing, it is worth noting the point at which the greatest lift is to be found. This is called the *centre of pressure* and it will be seen that this will move as the angle of attack is increased. The importance of the lift derived from the angle of attack can be seen when an aircraft is flying upside down. The cambered upper surface is in the wrong place, but the aircraft continues to gain or lose height, and to travel through the air. Some military aircraft, in fact, have symmetrically curved wings so that they can fly equally well upside down and the correct way up.

However efficient a wing may be, it cannot avoid creating drag as well as lift. If a shape is placed into a flow of air it is bound to create a disturbance however streamlined the shape may be. Profile drag is the name given to the disturbance caused by the presence of the wing in the airflow but there is another type too – induced drag. This is caused by the high pressure beneath the wing trying to reach the lower pressure above. As the airflows from the top and bottom of the wing meet at the tip, vortexes are set up – whirling trails of air which can be very powerful (figure 4). The separation of airliners as they take off and land is necessary because of the wake of turbulence which trails from the wing tips. If there is too close a gap between the aircraft, the trailing air could cause a following airliner to topple out of control from the sky.

There are many different wing shapes and each has a particular job to do. A straight thick wing, for example, will provide good lift but also quite a lot of drag. Such a wing is more often to be found on short-range aircraft which serve small airports. Their slow flying capabilities enable them to land on short runways which faster aircraft could not manage. Until the advent of the jet age, all airliners had straight wings. Even the largest of piston engines could only power airliners to certain speeds. Any further increase in speed depended upon the jet engine and a more efficient wing.

Fig. 4 Airflows from the top and bottom of the wing mix and produce vortices.

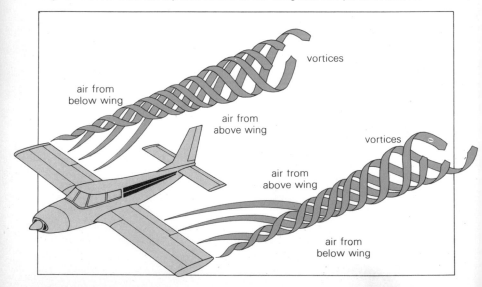

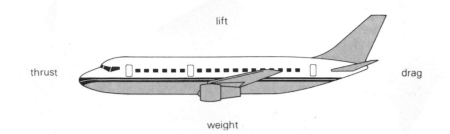

lift

thrust

drag

weight

Opposite forces provide problems for aircraft designers who have produced many different shapes to fit different aircraft types for particular tasks.

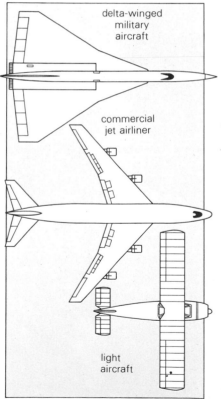

delta-winged
military
aircraft

commercial
jet airliner

light
aircraft

The jet engine brought the capability of increasing airliner speeds from about 520km/h to over 930km/h but before this was possible, something had to be done about wing drag. Remember that the airflow over the top of the wing moves much faster than that below. One consequence of this is that at high speeds the shock waves associated with supersonic flight begin to build up on the upper surface of the wing. Aircraft designers found that the solution to this problem was to 'sweep' the wing. This helped considerably to delay the build-up of 'sonic' shock waves by effectively increasing the 'chord' – the distance between the leading and trailing edges of the wing. By reducing the camber on the wing as well, the build-up of the sonic shock wave is further delayed. For by slowing down the airflow over the top of the wing, greater speeds are possible, although this increased speed is at the expense of lift.

45

The distinctive shape of the Concorde marks a step in the progress of air transport.
Singapore airlines operate a joint service with British Airways to the Far East.

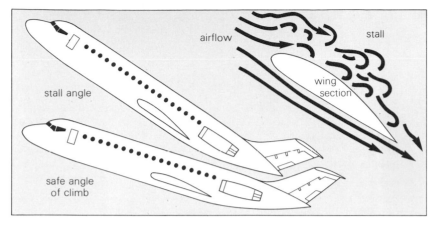

Fig. 5 Pilots must be careful to climb at the correct attitude to avoid a stall.

These examples cover the two extremes of airliner design; the thick, straight wing giving plenty of lift but less speed and the thin, swept wing capable of much higher speeds but providing rather less lift. There are of course many other wing designs which are produced for particular tasks, such as the delta of the Concorde. This has a very complicated shape with not only a very wide chord but varying degrees of sweep resulting in an Ogee or 'wine-glass' form. The Concorde wing has to make a number of compromises, the most important of which is to perform efficiently both at twice the speed of sound and at the much lower landing speeds at the end of a journey. A slender delta wing can be relatively thin, permitting high speeds, and at the same time provide a large wing area to contain the large quantities of fuel needed for supersonic flight.

We have noted that the centre of pressure changes its position as the angle of attack is altered. The ultimate effect of this is a very serious condition known as the stall. Figure 5 shows what happens when the wing assumes too steep an angle. The centre of pressure has moved to the leading edge of the wing and instead of a smooth flow over the upper surface there is a great deal of turbulent air. Consequently lift has been lost and the aircraft can no longer fly. It goes without saying that a stall must be avoided at all costs – especially at such critical points in a flight as the take-off and landing.

Many devices have been produced to provide additional lift when the aircraft is flying relatively slowly. We have seen that a stall occurs when there is no longer a smooth flow of air over the wing. Such a condition will be brought about by climbing at an 'impossible' angle or by having insufficient forward speed. As the wing of a high speed airliner is shaped to be at its most efficient at high speeds, we obviously are going to have problems at low speeds unless we do something about it. The Concorde is exceptional in being able to fly at high angles of attack without stalling, but a conventional airliner has a wing designed for high sub-sonic speeds. There is very little margin for error when flying a swept-wing airliner; if the correct speed is not maintained or the aircraft is put into too steep a climb, a stall will result, usually with disastrous results.

The dangers of stalling were soon discovered in the early days of flying and various remedies have since been devised to delay the stall as long as possible. One method is to fit slats to the leading edge of the wing. These pop out automatically when the centre of pressure moves forward with the approach of the stall. A gap is created between the slat and the main wing so that a smooth airflow can be maintained (figure 6).

Another device for changing the shape of the wing is the flap. There are many different types of flap but they all have a two-fold purpose: to provide additional lift by extend-

Fig. 6 Spoilers on the wing work with the flaps to slow the airliner when it lands.

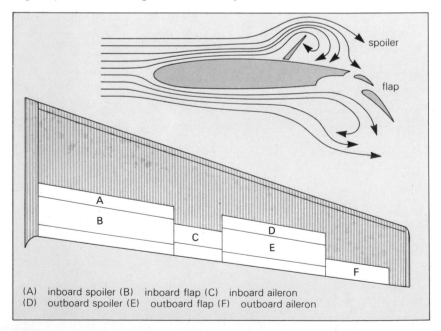

(A) inboard spoiler (B) inboard flap (C) inboard aileron
(D) outboard spoiler (E) outboard flap (F) outboard aileron

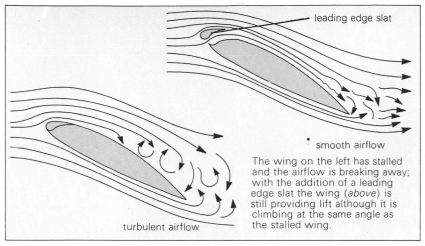

leading edge slat

smooth airflow

The wing on the left has stalled and the airflow is breaking away; with the addition of a leading edge slat the wing (*above*) is still providing lift although it is climbing at the same angle as the stalled wing.

turbulent airflow

Wing slats reduce the stall speed of an aircraft.

ing the curve on the upper wing surface and to add drag and therefore lower the speed during landing. Some airliners, such as the Boeing 727, are equipped with flaps on the leading and trailing edges; when they are all employed it may look to some as if the wing is falling apart! However, the devices enable the aircraft to take off and land in relatively short distances and at reasonably slow speeds. Without the aid of flaps, modern jet airliners would have to land at dangerously high speeds and miles of runway would be necessary for the aircraft to reach take-off speed.

Although perhaps the most important and complicated part of an aeroplane, the wing is of course only one component; power is necessary to push the wing through the air to obtain lift. A fuselage is also necessary – not least to make the whole thing worthwhile by carrying passengers! Finally a tail has to be fitted to provide stability, and various controls attached so that the aircraft can be manoeuvred about the sky.

Just as the wing has a centre of pressure applying lift in one direction, so Mother Earth ensures that there is a pull in the opposite direction – gravity. Every aircraft has what is termed the centre of gravity, the fulcrum on which the aircraft is balanced. Unfortunately, the centre of gravity does not remain in a single position. The addition of passengers, cargo and fuel may slightly alter the balance of the aircraft and, as we have seen, the centre of pressure can move to bring about a further change. If the aircraft is to be stable and not pitch wildly up and down, something has to be done to ensure that the centre of pressure and the centre of gravity remain balanced (figure 7). The solution to the problem is to fit a tailplane at the end of the fuselage. Although this looks like a miniature wing, it is not designed to produce lift when the aircraft is level. Usually the tailplane has an equal camber on the upper and lower surfaces so that, should the nose pitch up, the tailplane will provide momentary lift to bring the aircraft back to a horizontal position. This is called longitudinal stability. What if the pilot should want to pitch the nose up – to climb for example? To provide movement in pitch, the tailplane is fitted with elevators – one of the three principle means of controlling the aircraft. As the pilot pulls the control column back, the elevator is raised into the airstream which promptly tries to pull it down. As the tail of the aircraft goes down, of course, the nose must rise.

The aircraft will need to change direction as well as climb and descend. For this manoeuvre ailerons are fitted to the trailing edge of the outer wing. These enable the pilot to roll the aircraft in the direction he wishes to turn. With the aircraft banked a proportion of the lift generated by the wing is acting in the direction in which the aircraft is required to turn.

In order to avoid the aircraft sideslipping during the turn the third control surface, a rudder, is fitted to the fin. Like the tailplane, the fin and rudder have a symmetrical airfoil – the camber is equal on both sides. Also like the tailplane, the fin provides stability–directional stability. All the controls act 'naturally'; a pull on the column and the nose will rise and the aircraft will climb. Move the column to the left and the aircraft will bank to the left, aided by the rudder as the pilot pushes the left pedal.

Fig. 7 The tailplane, fin and rudder provide a vital balance and longitudinal stability.

rudder

fin

tail plane

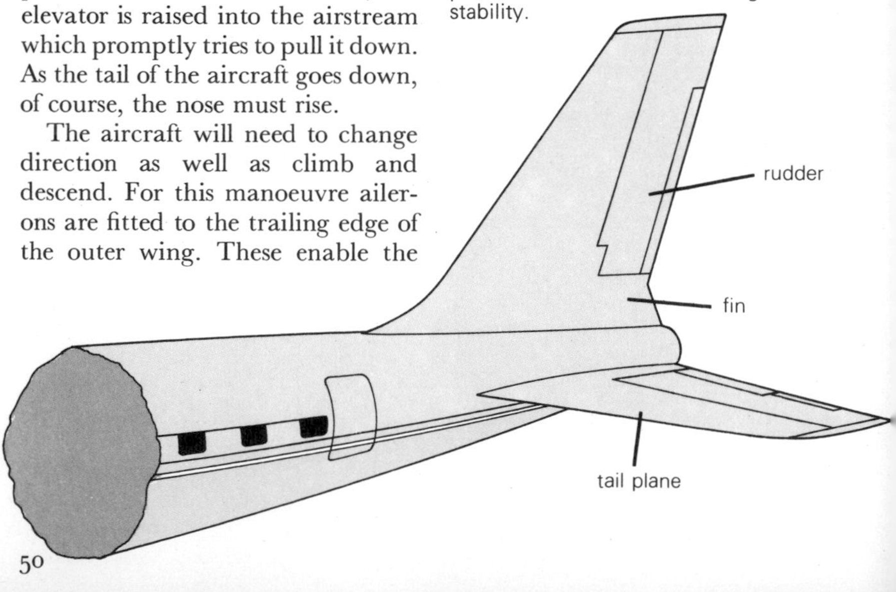

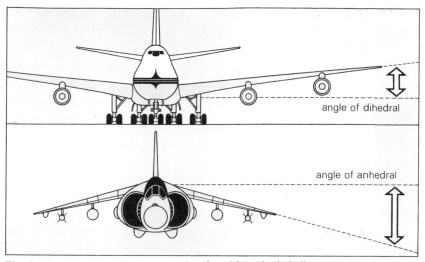

Fig. 8 Wing dihedral helps keep an aircraft stable; anhedral allows an aircraft to be quickly manoeuvred about the sky.

Before moving on to describe further controls, mention must be made of another fundamental aspect of aircraft design which adds to stability. We have seen that longitudinal and directional stability are provided by the fin and tailplane. In order to prevent the aircraft from waggling uncomfortably from side to side, the wings are tilted up slightly so that the tips are higher than the root (figure 8). This is called dihedral and because an airliner's wings are flexible, it is often only possible to see this when the aircraft is in the air. How does wing dihedral stop the aircraft rolling, or achieve what is called lateral stability? It must be remembered that the pull of gravity is always downwards, regardless of the attitude of

the aircraft, so that if one wing should drop, the aircraft will slip sideways. The lower wing will momentarily provide more lift than the higher wing because it is slipping into the airflow. The upper wing is both shielded by the fuselage and is providing less lift; it will therefore drop, bringing the aircraft back on to an even keel. The fin and the fuselage also help to keep the aircraft level because, in a sideslip, the airflow will push against them.

However in the case of some aircraft with a high proportion of in-built stability – as with a high wing aircraft – or in military types requiring high manoeuvrability a de-stabilising influence may be introduced by using anhedral – the wings pointing down at the tips.

A modern airliner

(1) Two pilots and a flight engineer control the flight of this Jumbo.

(2) The lounge of the first-class cabin enables passengers to relax during a long journey.

(3) The weather radar gives an advanced warning of storms and other hazards.

(4) The under belly of the Boeing 747 can carry more cargo than a Boeing 707 freighter.

(5) Meals for up to 400 passengers are prepared and served from the galleys.

(6) Leading edge slats provide additional lift during take-off and landing.

(7) Powerful engines provide over 50,000 lb. thrust.

(8) The flaps enable the Jumbo to reduce speed for landing. They also provide extra lift during take-off.

(9) The undercarriage is neatly stowed after retraction

(10) Well over 400 passengers can be accom-modated in the capacious cabin of the 747.

In a 747 'Jumbo' jet hundreds of people may be travelling thousands of miles, and they will be on board the aircraft for hours at a stretch. To transport them safely and comfortably the aircraft must be a complex and highly sophisticated machine.

(11) In an emergency, escape chutes are inflated at the exits so that the passengers can slide to safety.

(12) Up to three different films can be shown in the various cabins although often one cabin is set aside for those who prefer to read or work.

(13) Powerful ailerons control the direction of flight.

(14) The pressure bulkhead ensures that the cabin pressure is kept comfortable.

(15) A mini-jet engine (the auxiliary power unit) generates power for the aircraft when it is on the ground.

Having declared that, as far as basic principles are concerned, all aircraft are the same, it is time to confess that there are nevertheless some major differences too. Certainly the pilot of a light aircraft uses the same control system as that of a DC-10 or Trident. However just as the driver of a Mini would find a 10-tonne truck a bit of a handful, so a novice pilot would soon find that a jet airliner was more than he could handle safely and efficiently.

A brief description of a flight in a light aircraft may help to set the scene for the activity on the flight deck of a larger airtransport 'plane. It has been said that anyone who can drive a car could also learn to fly an aeroplane. Certainly many young people have acquired flying skills at an early age – often before they are old enough to hold a full flying licence. Alas it is very expensive to fly privately and most enthusiasts have to content themselves with watching aircraft from the ground.

Before climbing aboard an aircraft – in this case, let's say a Piper Cherokee – a pilot will carry out an inspection to make sure that the oil level is correct and there is fuel in the tank. A host of detailed checks follows: tyres, flaps, radio aerials, the propeller, etc. When he is satisfied that the aircraft is safe to fly, the pilot takes his seat – and begins another series of checks. Reading from a printed card, he must satisfy

himself that everything is ready before he starts the engine; the fuel tank is selected and the battery master switch is turned on. At the press of a button the engine fires into life and, as it warms up, yet more checks are carried out. If any instrument shows that the engine is not working properly or some other vital component is out of action, the pilot must shut down the motor and abandon the flight – safety is paramount.

When the pilot is satisfied that all is well, the correct frequency is selected on the radio and permission to taxi is requested. As the throttle is opened, the little aircraft moves forward and the checks continue as the brakes are tested. The aeroplane arrives at the runway, more checks are made, the engine is run at high power and the magnetos are checked; with the throttle closed, the slow running of the engine should reveal any suspicious roughness. The trimmer is set to neutral for take off and the instruments are again checked, the control tower is asked by the pilot for permission for the aircraft to take off. The aircraft is lined up on the runway, the throttle is fully opened and with a roar the Cherokee gathers speed. Taking care to steer a straight course using the rudder – a cross-wind might cause the aircraft to veer off the runway – the pilot keeps an eye on the air speed indicator (ASI) and at 70 mph gently eases the 'wheel' or 'stick' back. As the aircraft climbs

Above 'Home-built' aircraft are a source of great enjoyment for many aviation enthusiasts. *Below* A line-up of Rollason Condors.

into the air an eagle eye is maintained on the ASI, remembering that too steep a climb will result in a loss of speed and the possibility of a stall. On reaching his cruising height of 2000 ft the pilot eases the throttle back and builds the speed up to about 120 mph in level flight.

Whilst it is very pleasant to enjoy a bird's-eye view of the ground, the pilot must remain alert, watching for other aircraft and monitoring the instruments. For, should something go wrong, a careful pilot will be ready for an emergency. The discipline of the checks which begins even before the pilot takes a seat in the aeroplane is designed to make flying safe and, sure enough, our sample flight is without incident. Our pilot is even sitting without his hands on the control wheel, having

trimmed the aircraft for level flight. The Cherokee – like many airliners – has an 'all flying' tail instead of elevators on the tail, and the trimmer adjusts the tail so that it is in the best position for take-off, cruising and landing. Turning a handle on the 'ceiling', the pilot can feel if he has trimmed the aircraft correctly; in level flight the Cherokee will not need constant adjustment of the control wheel. Conversely, if the aircraft is incorrectly trimmed the elevator (or all-flying tail) will feel very heavy and will make control difficult.

As our Cherokee pilot ends his short flight, he requests the tower's permission to rejoin the airfield's circuit and carries out more checks in preparation for his landing. Joining the queue of other aircraft

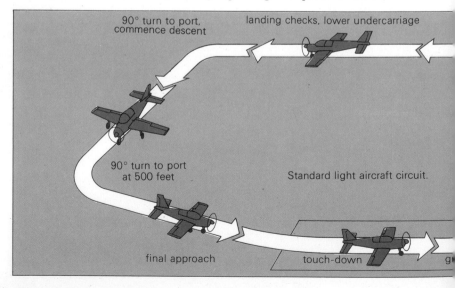

90° turn to port, commence descent

landing checks, lower undercarriage

90° turn to port at 500 feet

Standard light aircraft circuit.

final approach

touch-down

g

Above Training aircraft like this Cherokee have well-equipped instrument panels.

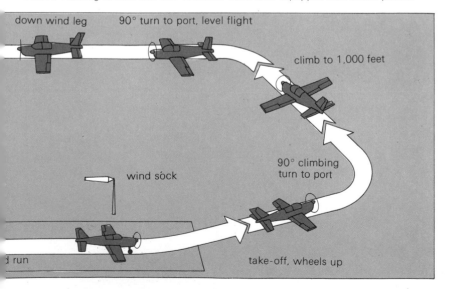

down wind leg   90° turn to port, level flight

climb to 1,000 feet

wind sock

90° climbing
turn to port

d run

take-off, wheels up

the pilot selects his flaps so that he can fly safely and slowly as he approaches the runway. A landing is the most taxing demonstration of a pilot's skill and no two landings are alike. Once again a watchful eye is kept on the ASI as well as on the runway ahead. At a steady 75 mph the Cherokee is brought to a position just above the runway. Slowly the throttle is closed as the aircraft is held on a steady course and the wheels touch the runway – hopefully, but not always, gently! Factors such as cross-winds or turbulence on the runway threshold can influence the landing and much of a pilot's training is devoted to mastering the skill of ending a flight safely.

It could well be that the captain

Chipmunks and Cherokees at Hamble College of Air Training, England.

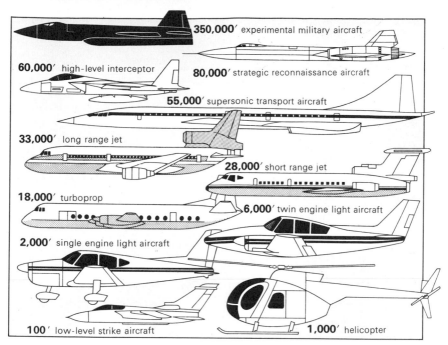

350,000′ experimental military aircraft

60,000′ high-level interceptor

80,000′ strategic reconnaissance aircraft

55,000′ supersonic transport aircraft

33,000′ long range jet

28,000′ short range jet

18,000′ turboprop

6,000′ twin engine light aircraft

2,000′ single engine light aircraft

100′ low-level strike aircraft

1,000′ helicopter

Above Different kinds of aircraft cruise at different heights.

of a Trident or Boeing airliner at Heathrow began his flying career by learning on a Cherokee. The Oxford Air Training School, for example, trains student pilots from many parts of the world and the lessons learned at such a school will be applied throughout a pilot's career.

Our 'flight' in a Cherokee has shown some aspects of flying which are common to all types of aircraft – not least the importance of carrying out checks. It is not unusual for about 170 items to be checked during the course of a flight. An airliner is controlled in exactly the same way as our Cherokee, except that it is far more complicated. There will be autopilots and other aids to flying which will baffle the novice pilot and the Inertial Navigation System displays a quite astonishing accuracy. In Chapter Five we will see these wonders in action; suffice to say that a 300-tonne airliner will not handle like a Cherokee. An airliner pilot must anticipate the action of his aircraft; for the greater weight of the airliner and the thinner air at which he flies cause some delay in the response to his commands.

90% of the mass of air is to be

59

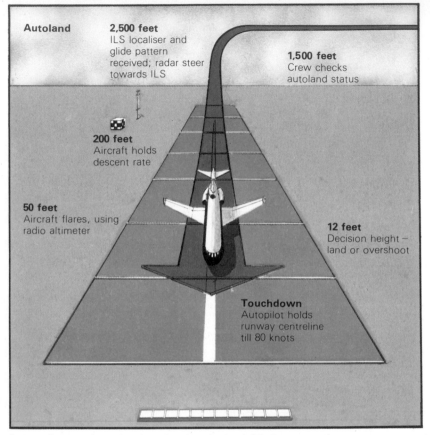

Autoland

2,500 feet
ILS localiser and
glide pattern
received; radar steer
towards ILS

1,500 feet
Crew checks
autoland status

200 feet
Aircraft holds
descent rate

50 feet
Aircraft flares, using
radio altimeter

12 feet
Decision height –
land or overshoot

Touchdown
Autopilot holds
runway centreline
till 80 knots

Automatic controls can enable aircraft to be landed in foggy weather.

found up to a height of some 15 km, the extent of the troposphere, one of three main layers surrounding the Earth. At the upper limits of the troposphere, temperatures fall to as low as −60°C, conditions very different from those experienced by our Cherokee pilot flying at a mere 2000 ft. Concorde regularly flies at 18·5 km above the Earth's surface,

its pilots using rudder pedals and a control wheel much as would be found on a Cherokee, but atmospheric conditions and the very high speeds of the aircraft ensure that there the similarity ends.

To ease the task of airline pilots, 'autopilots' have been under development since the 1920s. Using a gyroscope to sense movement, autopilots were originally designed to keep an aircraft on an even keel. If the aircraft begins to climb, the nose-up movement is detected by the gyroscope and a signal sent to a servopower unit which moves the flying control to push the nose down.

Gradually the skills of autopilots have been improved so that today they can be told to keep an aircraft on a particular course, at a prescribed height and speed. The automatic system on a TriStar, for instance, can even be used to land the aircraft – full autoland. Nowadays the pilot of an airliner uses the traditional control methods but because aircraft have become so large and fast, the control surfaces are moved mechanically. The controls on a Cherokee can be easily moved by human muscle-power alone but the massive control surfaces of a modern airliner would be beyond the strength of the burliest pilot. So powered flying controls are fitted to present-day airliners; the pilot's instructions are conveyed to the controls by a system of hydraulic 'muscles'. To avoid a potential disaster caused by the failure of a hydraulic motor or a leaking pipe, the powered control system may be triplicated or even quadruplicated. Because the controls will do as they are told by the pilot without protest, artificial feel is fed into the system.

Gyroscopes at the 'nerve centre' of the autopilot activate servopower units.

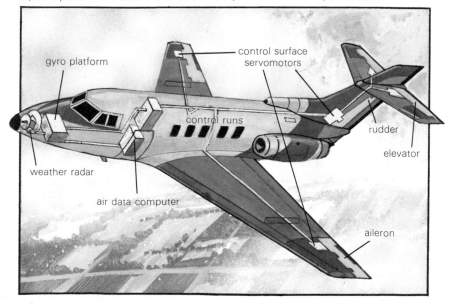

gyro platform

control surface
servomotors

control runs

rudder

elevator

weather radar

air data computer

aileron

This enables the pilot to control the aircraft in exactly the same way as a manual system; should one of the controls feel particularly heavy, the pilot will be warned that he must take some action.

Gradually, mechanical controls are giving way to electrical systems – called 'Fly-by-wire'. Electrical controls are much lighter than mechanical designs and are more accurate. Before long, active controls will become a feature of tomorrow's airliners. These are not designed to take over control from the pilot but rather to make flying more comfortable for the passengers and bring other benefits. A compu-ter on board will send instructions to the flying controls so that they take almost immediate action when a gust causes the aircraft to roll or bump. Sometimes an air journey can be very uncomfortable because turbulent air tosses the aircraft about the sky. Active controls will do much to alleviate the uncomfort-able 'bumps' and to make for a smooth flight.

As a further aid to airline pilots, many aircraft are fitted with spoilers or lift dumpers. Normally retracted to lie flat on the top surface of the wing, they can be raised to slow the aircraft during a steep descent. When the airliner touches down on

Commander C. R. Samson, R.N., a British aviation pioneer.

The Boeing 747 has a complicated flap arrangement to get the maximum efficiency from the wing.

the runway the spoilers are fully raised to reduce the lift provided by the wing and keep the aircraft firmly on the runway. On some aircraft the spoilers can be used differentially, for roll control, instead of the ailerons. On some high-speed airliners the ailerons are situated not only at the wing-tips, but also about midway between the wing-root and the tip.

We have seen that in order to fly an aeroplane needs wings and controls – it also, of course, needs power. The success of the Wright brothers' *Flyer* depended upon their development of a suitable piston engine. Both steam and petrol engines had been tried by some would-be aviators but, unable to find a suitable engine from any of the motor manufacturers, the Wrights built their own. Light weight and high power were the qualities needed to

power an aeroplane and the petrol-driven engine was developed to meet these requirements. For forty years it remained the principal means of powering aircraft. Bigger and bigger engines with more and more cylinders met the needs of aircraft designers until further development seemed almost impossible.

As early as the 1920s engine designers had considered other means of propelling aircraft. Technicians in Britain, Germany, Italy and other countries tried to produce a jet engine. There were some spectacular failures but successful engines were produced in both Britain and Germany during the Second World War and, of course, their first application was to warplanes. Some foresighted leaders in aviation, however, busied themselves in planning airliners which would be built after the war.

Following Sir Frank Whittle's success in producing a jet engine, several companies brought out their own designs. All employed the same basic principle: a large volume of air was compressed, passed to a combustion chamber and forced out of the rear of the engine through a turbine.

The early engines were not very powerful or reliable, leading some to regard the piston engine as safe from competition for many years. Such a view proved to be shortsighted as the hundreds of jet airliners at major airports today testify.

Jet engines may be listed under four categories: turbojet, turbofan, turboprop and turboshaft. The turbojet is the earliest form of jet engine which was used to power the first generation of jet airliners. In these engines almost all of the air which passes through the compressor is sent into the combustion chamber. The velocity of the hot gases emerging from the tailpipe is the principal source of noise as the aircraft thunders into the atmosphere. The turbojet was chosen to power Concorde because the thrust of a turbofan engine reduces at high altitudes, of the sort Concorde must attain to reach Mach 2. The turbojet also has a low frontal area – important in a sleek, very streamlined supersonic transport aircraft.

The turbofan is a 'by-pass' engine where only part of the air is fully compressed and passed into the combustion chamber. The rest of the air is sent around the hot combustion section to rejoin the heated air as it is pushed out by the turbine.

The inventor of the first aircraft jet engine to run was the British Sir Frank Whittle. But the German Heinkel He 178 was the first jet-powered aircraft to fly.

Jet engines are tested for thousands of hours before they are cleared for service.

The overall jet velocity is reduced and one consequence of this is a lower noise level. The 'big fans' used on the Jumbo and other wide-bodied aircraft have a high by-pass ratio. Although very powerful, such engines are also much quieter than earlier jets.

A turboprop has relatively little thrust but is designed instead to drive a propeller. The turbine is put to work driving a propeller which pulls the aircraft through the air. This type of engine is most efficient for relatively slow transport aircraft. The turboprop has all but ousted the piston engine as a power unit for propeller-driven transport aircraft.

The turboshaft is usually fitted to helicopters, driving the main and tail rotors through reduction gears.

Like the turboprop, it has little thrust from the exhaust.

As air traffic has grown, the noise caused by jet engines has become a major public issue. The efforts of manufacturers to reduce noise levels, however, are meeting with success as such giants as the Airbus demonstrate at airports throughout the world. Because of careful modification of the compressor design, the fitting of noise-absorbent linings and other measures, gradually the earth-shattering roar of jet engines is becoming a thing of the past.

An airliner's 'black box' records flight information and stores it in a strong, crash-proof box to help investigators should an accident happen. It is usually bright orange, not black, so it can be easily found.

Aircraft engines

The gas turbine has revolutionised all forms of aircraft — beginning with the fighter 'planes of the Second World War and reaching the pinnacle of achievement in the supersonic transport.

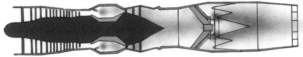

Above The Messerschmitt Me 262 fighter-bomber was powered by axial thrust jet engines. The air was compressed through several stages before entering the combustion chambers.

Below The Rolls-Royce Dart turbo-prop has a centrifugal gas turbine with a single compressor. It is very successful and economical and both drives a propeller and produces thrust.

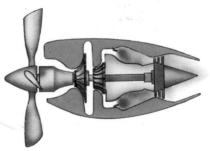

Left The big RB 211 turbofan is almost a turbo-prop — the large fan at the front compresses some of the air. This by-passes the rest of the air which is further compressed and passed into a combustion chamber.

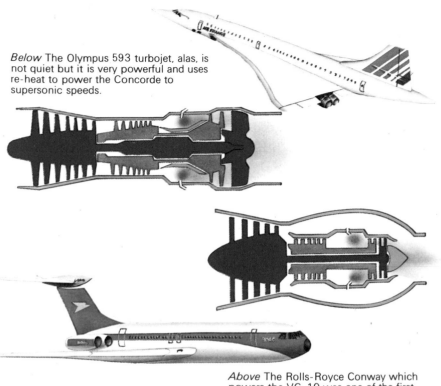

Below The Olympus 593 turbojet, alas, is not quiet but it is very powerful and uses re-heat to power the Concorde to supersonic speeds.

Above The Rolls-Royce Conway which powers the VC–10 was one of the first by-pass engines, with some of the air flowing over the combustion chamber.

Right A turboshaft engine like the Turbomeca Astazou which powers the Gazelle helicopter drives both the main and the tail rotors.

Airports-at the hub of the airways

Just as merchant ships plough their way along the sea lanes to ports where they load their cargoes so, too, hundreds of airliners wing their way to passenger and cargo terminals at the world's major airports.

The great seaports such as Liverpool and Rotterdam grew into cities as thousands of people became involved in the complexities of international trade. The 'ports' of the twentieth century have become almost like cities, too, needing thousands of people to look after the many facets of air travel.

The great seaports led to the growth of major cities. Some airports today have become small 'cities' in their own right.

Handling over 24 million passengers every year, London's Heathrow heads the league of international airports. The Chicago O'Hare airport tops the list for the highest number of aircraft movements (many small private 'planes add to the total), and handles over 40 million passengers annually – an incredible figure! But in terms of international airline movements, Heathrow is unchallenged. Clearly the geographical position of an airport influences the extent of its use. As Europe's southern 'gateway', Rome was at one point a very important airport for many airlines.

But the ability of modern airliners to fly long distances has tended to diminish the importance of that airport. As important trading nations, the United States, Germany, Japan and France attract many visitors and much air cargo. Consequently, New York, Frankfurt, Tokyo and Paris are amongst the busiest cities in terms of air traffic. To simplify the movement of passengers and cargo, a code has been devised so that airline staff the world over can communicate easily with one another. Baggage tagged by a porter in Bangkok (BKK) may be sent to Dusseldorf (DUS) via Istanbul

At the peak of the holiday season, airports can become very crowded, and aircraft congestion can lead to long delays.

(IST) and be handled by other porters and baggage loaders who will understand the codes. Where a city has only one major airport such as Hong Kong (HKG) and Brussels (BRU) the use of airport codes is uncomplicated but where there are several, such as in Paris and London, the destination airport must have its own code. LHR and LGW will enable a cargo handler to tell that boxes are destined for London/Heathrow and London/Gatwick. Similarly, the Paris airports of Orly, Le Bourget and Charles de Gaulle are known universally as ORY, LBG and CDG.

There are as many different types of airports as there are seaports. Although performing much the same task, the ports of Hamburg and Rotterdam have distinct characters of their own. So, too, airports differ considerably. The new Charles de Gaulle airport in Paris, for example, has a futuristic look about it which would not be out of place in a science fiction film. Passengers are conducted by 'travelators' (moving walkways) along tunnels to 'satellite' terminals and in the main building glass-topped tubes conduct the air travellers to the baggage hall.

Paris/Charles de Gaulle airport is one of the most modern in the world. These 'tubes' convey passengers from the arrival level to the baggage reclaim area.

No less modern, but run on quite a different principle, Montreal's Mirabel airport features mobile lounges which transport passengers between airliners and the terminal building. Many other airports have developed and grown over the years as demand has outstripped the facilities. Heathrow is just one such example. Starting in 1919 as a very rudimentary airstrip called Hounslow Heath, the airport came into its own at the end of the Second World War. Air traffic burgeoned as the world recovered from the destruction of war but for some time Heathrow consisted of no more than a motley collection of huts and tents on what is now the Northside. Some huts remain in use to this day but the development of the Central Area eventually led to the construction of three passenger terminals. It is interesting to see how terminal design at Heathrow has altered over the years. The brick-built Terminal Two was in fact the first to be erected and it was followed by Terminals Three and One (in that order). As traffic continued to grow, measures had to be taken to alleviate the pressure on Terminal Two. When it opened it handled all the European traffic, and long-distance flights continued to use the hutted facilities on the Northside. Terminal Three featured a much enlarged check-in area for the passengers, avoiding – at least for a while – some of the overcrowding of the first building. Terminal One was

built largely for the use of BEA (since merged with BOAC to become British Airways) and it too was designed to allow much more room for passengers to check in and get to their aircraft. The use of 'fingers' was another device which enabled the airport to handle larger numbers of aircraft and passengers. Long 'jetties' were built from the terminals so that more aircraft could be parked to unload their passengers.

Much thought has been devoted to airport planning but no one design has yet emerged as clearly superior to any other. Many architects and planners have striven to keep the distance between the entrance to the terminal and the door

Heathrow began post-war operations with a motley collection of huts and tents. The passenger check-in tent (*bottom*) provides a striking contrast to today's crowded terminals.

Airport terminals have had to handle a rapidly growing number of passengers as the popularity of air travel has increased.

of the airliner to an absolute minimum. Washington's Dulles International and Montreal's Mirabel airports have solved the problem by using mobile lounges, thus avoiding the need for long 'fingers'. Some, like Rio de Janeiro's Galeao airport and Cologne airport use a curved terminal building to bring the approach roads as close to the airport apron as possible. The old Berlin Tempelhof airport was a pioneer of this type of design, featuring a curved building with a canopy under which aircraft could load and unload their passengers.

Of course, not all airports have fine modern buildings: some continue to use terminals built in the 1930s. Indeed there are hundreds of airports dotted around the world where air traffic is not heavy enough to warrant a re-building programme. If there are only a dozen flights a day, there is no need for a grand (and expensive) terminal – a few huts or a single-storey building are usually quite adequate. Such terminals are to be found in all parts of the world and often have an intimate – and quite memorable – atmosphere.

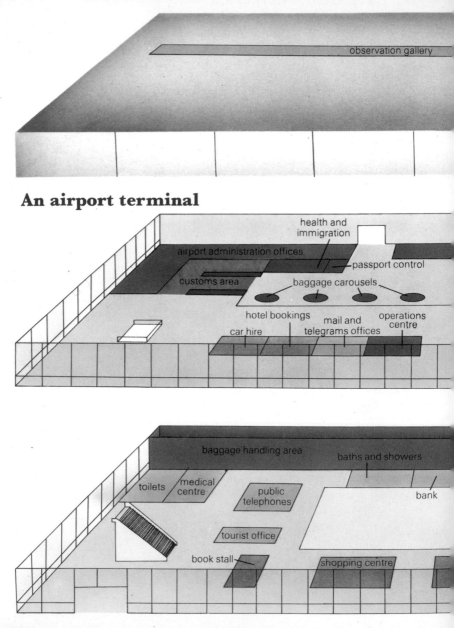

An airport terminal

observation gallery

health and
immigration

airport administration offices

passport control

customs area

baggage carousels

hotel bookings

car hire

mail and
telegrams offices

operations
centre

baggage handling area

baths and showers

toilets

medical
centre

public
telephones

bank

tourist office

book stall

shopping centre

74

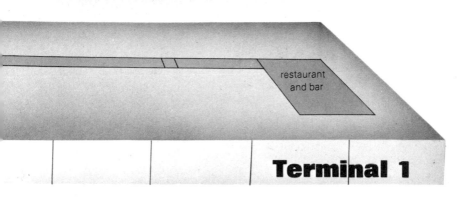

restaurant
and bar

Terminal 1

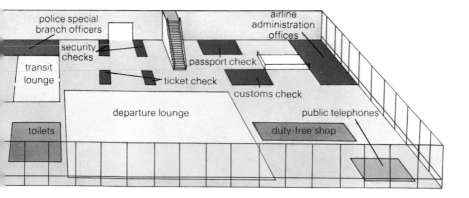

police special
branch officers

security
checks

transit
lounge

ticket check

airline
administration
offices

passport check

customs check

departure lounge

public telephones

toilets

duty-free shop

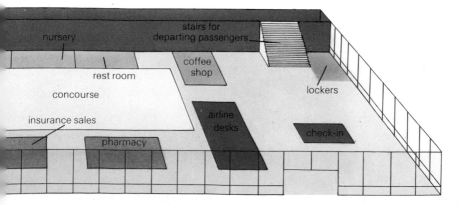

nursery

stairs for
departing passengers

coffee
shop

rest room

concourse

lockers

insurance sales

airline
desks

pharmacy

check-in

As traffic grows, however, planners have to consider ways of making airports more and more efficient. It is a seemingly never-ending task to process passengers as quickly as possible from the check-in desk to the aircraft. Once again computers have come to the aid of airline staff. An Airbus-load of passengers can involve checking in 280 people. (Remember that an airliner only earns its living when it is in the air.) As a passenger hands his ticket to the clerk at the check-in counter it is not simply a matter of tearing out the coupon and labelling the baggage for the right destination. The clerk must quickly scan the ticket to see if the correct fare has been charged, that it is still valid and that the booking has been made. The sample ticket coupon (figure 1) explains more clearly just what the clerk must check before he weighs the baggage, (noting it on the ticket), issues a receipt which is stuck on the ticket and pulls the coupon out. With the baggage labelled and sent on its way to be sorted on to the correct flight, the clerk then makes out a boarding pass, entering the selected seat number. An average of one and a half minutes per passenger is allowed for this operation. More time must be allowed for checking-in a passenger on a long distance flight. Visas and health certificates must be checked then, for many countries make airlines responsible if a passenger's documentation is not in

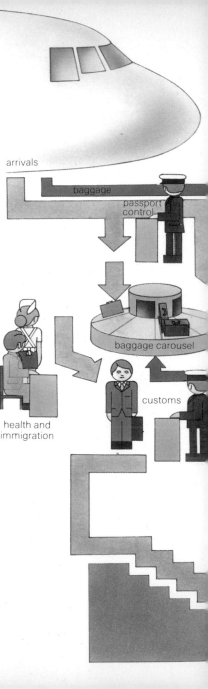

arrivals

baggage

passport control

baggage carousel

customs

health and immigration

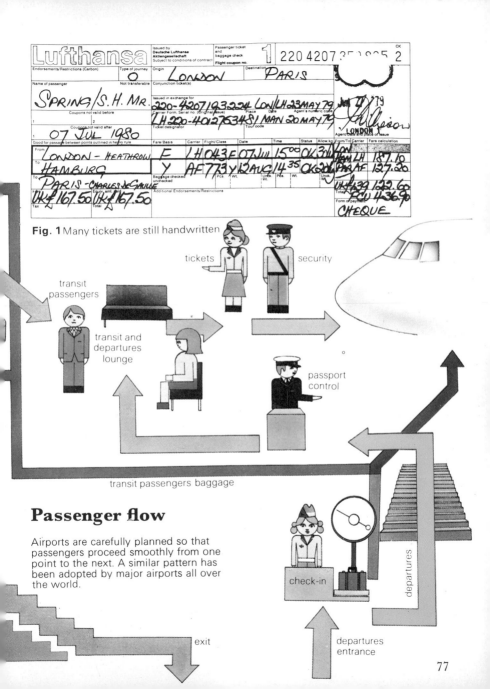

Fig. 1 Many tickets are still handwritten

tickets

security

transit passengers

transit and departures lounge

passport control

transit passengers baggage

Passenger flow

Airports are carefully planned so that passengers proceed smoothly from one point to the next. A similar pattern has been adopted by major airports all over the world.

check-in

departures

exit

departures entrance

order. Not only may the airline be obliged to fly the passenger back home on the next service but it may have to pay a substantial fine as well if papers are not in order. It is clear that the clerks at the desk have to work quickly and accurately with the ever-present stress of working under the impatient eyes of queuing passengers. Their colleagues at the ticket-counter need cool heads, too, as they issue tickets to passengers who may have only minutes to spare before the aircraft departs. Airline fares are complicated and staff have to receive special training in order to become expert in calculating the correct price. Thick manuals help them to reach the right conclusion but they have to remember many basic rules. An example of the type of 'map' used to calculate fares is shown in figure 2. In the days when the US dollar and pound sterling were strong currencies, fares were usually calculated in these currencies and then converted into the local currency. Nowadays the 'international' currencies fluctuate too much in value to be used for fare calculations, so the airlines have devised their own 'currency'. Called a Fare Calculation Unit (FCU) it is now the standard currency used when working out a fare. A conversion rate from FCUs into the local currency is an indispensible aid for the specialists who calculate fares. For many years international air fares have been controlled through IATA (International Air Transport Association). Most governments have approved of this arrangement, recognising that some order in the airline industry is necessary. For some airlines are not operated simply on a commercial basis but rather as a symbol of national prestige or as a means of earning foreign currency. To allow airlines to set their own fares could lead to damaging 'price wars' so the IATA rate-fixing has been allowed to continue – until recent years, that is.

The danger in allowing an association to fix fares is that airlines may become complacent, limiting competition to the prettiness of the hostesses or the standard of the meals. Non-IATA charter airlines have tended to undermine such complacency by offering much lower fares. A notable example of innovation in air transport is the Laker Skytrain service. By operating a simplified booking system and cutting out free meals, Laker provided a low cost service which soon became popular. The IATA airlines were obliged to reconsider their prices and they too offered 'standby' fares at greatly reduced rates. The IATA system of fixing fares has been attacked by the U.S. government which was never very happy to allow American airlines to take part in its fare arrangements. Under President Carter the U.S. government introduced a 'de-regulation' policy which allowed the American domestic carriers con-

Below Sir Freddie Laker. *Inset* Airline staff use complex diagrams to select routes.

Fig. 2.

siderable freedom to set their own fares. Encouraged by the success in their own country the Americans then set about trying to persuade other countries to adopt their methods. Many more routes into the United States were opened and more airlines joined the established trans-Atlantic and trans-Pacific carriers.

The IATA airlines were obliged to look anew at their fares system and many new rates were introduced. There has always been a bewildering variety of fares and airline staff dealing with fare calcu-lations sometimes have difficulty in working out the right rate. Fares may vary according to the season, the direction of travel, the age of the passenger, the time of the flight and the day of the week! There are special fares for travel agents, children, groups and students. The object of all these different fares is to fill as many seats on airliners as possible and to make the airlines profitable. Computers have not yet come to the aid of those who have to calculate fares but it is probably only a matter of time before this onerous task is given to an 'electronic brain'.

Computer reservations systems enable bookings to be handled in seconds. Messages to the central reservations control take only milliseconds.

Computers have long been used by major airlines to record passenger and cargo bookings. For years IATA airlines have used a common code called Airimp when making bookings. Not all airline computers can 'talk' to one another so the time-honoured system of telex communication is still often used. A coded language has been in use for many years to make this task easier. Imagine a request for a booking from the Mexico City offices of Lufthansa, outlining the intended journey of a passenger who wants to visit Leipzig in East Germany. With a single, 16-line message sent to several cities, not only could bookings be made on six different airlines, but hotel reservations could be made too. A trained clerk can read this code as easily as a secretary reads her shorthand. Frequent use soon enables the reservations clerks to get used to this strange language, the red and blue volumes of the ABC World Airways Guide being an indispensable aid on most airline ticket desks. As computer reservations systems become widely used, airline staff have had to learn to use the keyboards of computer terminals in place of the ballpoint pens and booking cards used previously. Messages can be flashed over immense distances in seconds; a counter-clerk in the British Airways' New York airline office typing out a booking request will receive a reply from the London computer in the twinkling of an eye. Computers have been taught to make out tickets, too: writing out tickets by hand is a laborious task but the computer can 'write out' a ticket in seconds. Figure 1 shows just how complicated a ticket can be and is a further example of the need for thorough training for airline staff.

Validity From	To	Days of Service	Dep	Arr	Flight No.	Stops Acft Class
FROM LONDON UK (LON) CONTINUED						
DENPASAR (DPS)						
F		FCU 1429.50	UKL 746.00			Max 10138
Y		880.80	459.50			
-	- 1	0815 LHR	1015 AMS	KL120	D9S	Y
		1200 AMS	*1430 HLP	KL831.	D10	FY
		*1630 HLP	*1815	GA686	DC9	FY
-	- 3	0815 LHR	1015 AMS	KL120	D9S	Y
		1200 AMS	*1300 HLP	GA891.	D10	FY
		*1630 HLP	*1815	GA686	DC9	FY
-	- 4	0815 LHR	1015 AMS	KL120	D9S	Y
		1200 AMS	*1455 HLP	GA895.	D10	FY
		*1630 HLP	*1815	GA686	DC9	FY
-	- 4	0815 LHR	1015 AMS	KL120	D9S	Y
		1200 AMS	*1445 HLP	KL833.	D10	FY
		*1630 HLP	*1815	GA686	DC9	FY
-	- 6	0815 LHR	1015 AMS	KL120	D9S	Y
		1200 AMS	*1415 HLP	KL835.	D10	FY
		*1630 HLP	*1815	GA686	DC9	FY
-	- 7	0815 LHR	1015 AMS	KL120	D9S	Y
		1200 AMS	*1455 HLP	GA893.	D10	FY
		*1630 HLP	*1815	GA686	DC9	FY
-	- 2	0905 LHR	*0700 BKK	TG911.	D10	FY
		*0800 BKK	*1435	TG423	D8S	FY
-	- 5	0905 LHR	*0715 BKK	TG913.	D10	FY
		*0800 BKK	*1435	TG423	D8S	FY

This extract from the ABC Airways Guide shows codes which must be learned.

Check-in staff must 'process' a passenger in a matter of a few minutes.

With his boarding pass at the ready, our passenger must now join the queues which form at the security screening and immigration desks. As air piracy has become a method of applying blackmail it is necessary to check every passenger in case he (or she) is carrying weapons. X-ray equipment and devices capable of 'sniffing' explosives are used to ensure that dangerous items may not be carried on board aircraft. The security staff are carefully trained to watch for signs which may betray a terrorist. The tension of someone carrying a hand-grenade will become clear to an experienced security officer as the line of passengers moves slowly towards the search area. After the security check, the immigration officer will want to see the passport of our passenger, checking to see that it is not out of date and watching out for forgeries. Once our passenger has assured the authorities that he is no criminal on the run, he is free to enter the departure lounge. Here the duty-free shops, bookstalls and souvenir counters tempt tourists to part with foreign currency for which they have no further use. They are no less popular with businessmen who welcome the opportunity to avoid paying duty. When the time comes to board the aircraft, a further security check is often made before the passengers finally file aboard.

Many airlines maintain comfortable lounges for their important passengers. These are quiet havens of peace away from the bustling crowds in the departure lounge, where businessmen may study their papers or relax before embarking.

At Lufthansa's staff training school a counter clerk practises her skill in front of a television camera. Her 'performance' will afterwards be discussed with an instructor.

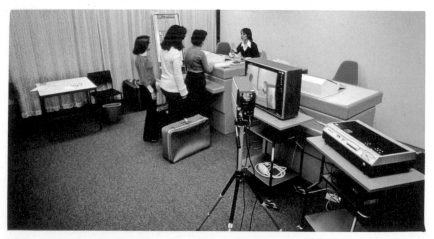

Above Security screening. X-ray machines and metal detectors are commonly used.
Below An airport duty-free shop.

The airport authorities, too, have their own VIP lounges for the use of diplomats, guests of the government, etc. Heads of State and other important dignitaries use a separate lounge at Heathrow. Far away from the crowded public terminals, it is on the south side of the airport where visiting 'bizjets' (small executive aircraft) are parked. Restaurants and coffee shops look after the physical needs of both passengers and visitors, whilst spiritual needs are not forgotten either. Many airports have a chapel where people of any denomination can sit in quiet contemplation. The bigger airports boast a variety of shops and services to cater for the needs of the airport staff and passengers.

As the well-oiled system processes passengers from the check-in counter to the aircraft cabin, many airline and airport workers are busy behind the scenes. The operations office of an airline co-ordinates all the essential services which must be carried out during the 'turn-round' of an airliner *(see page 102)*.

Most airports have several restaurants and bars (*below*) and also V.I.P. lounges (*above*).

Above Fresh meals are delivered. *Below* Passenger baggage.

When an airliner 'docks' a customs officer is one of the first aboard and when he is satisfied that all is in order (and the seals are on the store of duty-free liquor), the passengers are allowed to leave. Almost immediately cleaners come on board to tidy away rubbish and clean the cabin. Toilet and food waste is removed by special vehicles, whilst cargo and baggage are off-loaded. Often a giant tanker will be in attendance to pump tons of fuel on board, enough for the planned journey and some more for safety. From the airline kitchens fresh meals are delivered in easily handled containers which are of a standard size world-wide. Newspapers and magazines are placed on board and fresh soap, eau de cologne, etc., are placed in the toilets. Only when all details are correct can the new 'plane-load of passengers be allowed aboard. The growl of the GPU (Ground Power Unit) has been a

dominating sound since the airliner's arrival, for it provides the power to operate the aircraft's electrical system and may be used to start the engines when all the other service vehicles have departed. Some airliners dispense with the services of a GPU by using an APU (Auxiliary Power Unit), a small jet engine on the aircraft which can often be heard whistling above the heads of passengers as they climb on board. In this time of fuel conservation, however, using a GPU is sometimes preferred to running an APU for an hour during turn-round.

The 'Ops Room' co-ordinates all aspects of the flight from providing a wheel-chair for a sick passenger to looking after a young schoolboy travelling alone. Unaccompanied children are often very experienced travellers but the airlines have to take care of their young charges until a parent or other adult collects the globe-trotting passenger. Minor repairs notified by the crew are dealt with, and fuelling and replenishment of the aircraft's equipment are organised. The need for speed is paramount. For in organising the turn-round of an airliner the Station Manager and his staff are aware that a punctual departure is vital. Air traffic control, having been notified of the aircraft's Flight Plan, will have allocated a departure 'slot' at a particular time. If for some reason the airliner is not ready to leave at the appropriate time, it will miss its slot and may have to wait before another becomes available. It is small wonder that an Operations Room is often the scene of frantic activity followed by a lull after the airliner has left. As the powerful tug pushes the airliner away from the terminal (just like an ocean liner being manoeuvred from a jetty), the whole process starts again with the arrival of another aircraft. Each airline maintains an operations office and this busy scene is repeated all over the airport.

Cargo has become a major aspect of present-day airline operations. For years air cargo had been largely limited to a fill-up for passenger services, providing welcome extra revenue but only if the passenger load was light enough to permit some packages to be put on board. Nowadays all-cargo aircraft carry thousands of tonnes each year. Valu-

A disabled passenger is brought to a BAC 1-11 by an ambulance.

Powerful tugs are needed to manoeuvre airliners into position.

able loads can be carried without the need for elaborate packaging. Indeed, in terms of value Heathrow is one of Britain's most important 'ports', ahead even of Liverpool and Southampton. Many airports have built special cargo terminals or, in the case of Heathrow, a 'village' of cargo terminals. Once more our old friend the computer has come to the aid of the air cargo business. Bookings are handled by the airline's computers; the complicated paperwork associated with international shipments is processed by a computer and the handling of cargo within the terminal is controlled by – a computer, of course! Consignments large and small are delivered to the terminal and, like a giant postal sorting office, all the items are channelled to the right place. There they are loaded into containers, placed on to pallets or loaded directly into the aircraft. Everything from live pigs to a ship's propeller-shaft can be carried, the giant Boeing 747 freighter swallowing cargo through its nose beneath a raised section which looks like a knight's visor. A system of rails and points moves the containers.

There is enough space beneath the passenger cabins of such airliners as the DC-10, Airbus, TriStar and Boeing 747 to accommodate great quantities of cargo and the days when this type of business was the 'Cinderella' of the airlines have long since gone.

Cargo operations

cargo
warehouse

hinged
nose door

land-sea-air
container

loading
ramp

baggage containers

cargo containers

By the 1950s air cargo had become an important part of BEA's activity. Pepsi-Cola machines are seen (*below*) being loaded on to a DC-3 for a flight from London to Jersey.

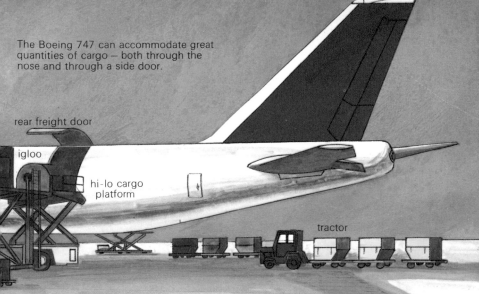

The Boeing 747 can accommodate great quantities of cargo — both through the nose and through a side door.

rear freight door

igloo

hi-lo cargo platform

tractor

The brain-child of Freddie Laker, the Carvair (*top left*) is a conversion of the DC-4. The swing-tail CL-44 cargo aircraft (*top right*) is another purpose-built aircraft which can be loaded with ease. Many airports have special cargo terminals (*bottom left*) which are used exclusively by freight aircraft, and specially designed trucks which raise loads to the correct level for loading into the belly of a jumbo (*bottom right*).

89

Before the use of radio became widespread, air traffic control was very rudimentary; flags or lamps were used to signal instructions to pilots. Burning flares lined the runway, which was often no more than a grass strip. By the 1930s, air traffic had grown sufficiently for the need for stricter control. It was no longer possible to allow airliners to find their own way (by following railway lines, for example). Air lanes were drawn between major cities and this system has remained the basis of air traffic control ever since. Previously the lanes were given the name of a colour, but the tendency in recent years has been to use the international alphabet and numbers instead. Thus Amber-One has become Alpha-One – for the standardization of practices is of vital importance to those who fly the airways of many countries. It is possible to fly

outside controlled airspace but it is usually helicopters, and executive, military and private aircraft which fly well away from the busy air lanes. Even outside controlled airspace there are still many rules to observe. Maps used by these pilots show many areas where flying is not permitted; nuclear research stations, firing ranges, military airfields, these and many more are indicated by shaded areas on the maps. They warn pilots that they must alter course.

The radar controllers in the approach control room 'police' large areas by watching the airliners on their radar screens. To the casual observer the many 'blips' on the radar scopes look alarmingly difficult to identify. Imagine the task of controlling air traffic at New York where several airports, and military and manufacturers' airfields are located quite close together. With great skill the controllers guide their unseen charges to the right place along the airways. Transponders carried on the airliners provide instant identification on the radar screen and computers can monitor the situation, automatically issuing a warning if two aircraft are set on a collision course.

A simple and reliable aid to air traffic control has been in use for many years. A paper strip bearing the essential details of each flight is fed in sequence to the air traffic controllers. Nowadays the paper strips are printed by a computer instead of being handwritten, but the concept remains the same. Both in the tower where controllers look after movements in the immediate vicinity of the airport, and in the approach control room, assistants feed the controllers with the strips. As the aircraft leaves the area of one controller to enter another, the appropriate strip is removed from one controller's panel to the next. Clearly one controller cannot look after all the lanes approaching the airport so responsibility is shared between several controllers, each sitting before a radar scope. It is a demanding and very responsible task.

The eye-catching control tower at ~~Dallas~~ DULLES Airport, WASHINGTON

Of course, air traffic control has many other facets. The aircraft must be controlled on the ground so that they take their place in an orderly queue for take-off. On the biggest airports a series of lights on the taxi-ways guides the pilots to the correct position for take-off or, conversely, to their parking places after they have landed. White markings on the runway help to tell the pilot how far he has to go when he is roaring along on his take-off run. They provide a warning in good time that there is a certain distance to go before the airliner will run out of concrete. Some 'overrun' accidents have happened because water on the runway has caused skidding.

It is possible for a thin film of water to bring about aquaplaning, making it impossible for an aircraft's brakes to work properly. A cure has been found which consists of many tiny grooves cut into the concrete. It has been found that such grooves are sufficient to drain the runway of water.

asphalt surface

It can be difficult for a pilot to find his way around a big airport at night. Lights in the centre of the taxiway help to guide the pilots to the correct position.

taxiway turn-off

runway visual range (RVR) points

layers of concrete

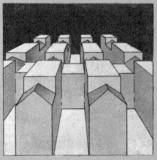

concrete sections which can be seeded with grass but will not be eroded by jet blast

Mother Nature has, alas, many other hazards to make the take-off and landing difficult. Fog can bring an airport to a halt. Even a shallow bank of fog may make forward visibility impossible for the air-crews. Instruments set up alongside the runway provide an accurate indication of Runway Visual Range (RVR). Usually given in metres, RVR will tell a pilot if he can attempt a landing or must divert to another airport. (Remember that extra fuel loaded for just such an eventuality?) Ice and snow are other hazards which some airport authorities must handle. Expensive specialised vehicles may remain unused for nine months of the year but will occasionally be called upon to clear the runways of snow. Sweepers, scrapers and blowers all combine to remove snow which could otherwise cause the airport to be closed. In such countries as Canada, where snow conditions last for many months, dye is sprayed on to the banks of snow which line the runways and taxi-tracks. When the ground is covered in a carpet of snow it is very difficult to see the edge of the runway.

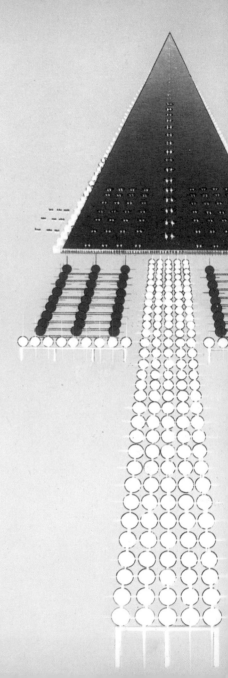

Airfield lighting must be reliable, easy to see and sometimes tough enough to withstand a landing airliner. The centreline lights, edge lights and approach lights can be varied in intensity to cope with changing visibility. Snow lights are mounted to rise above the snow level. Raised lights are designed to snap off if hit by an aircraft.

Centreline lights

Snow lights

Runway edge lights

Threshold lights

Visual
Approach
Slope
Indicator

Approach light

Airport lighting has progressed considerably since the days of the oil 'goose neck' lamps. A series of white lights marks the approach to the runway, and the runway itself is edged with lights at regular intervals. The centre-line of the runway is also marked by white lines set in metal housings at the same level as the concrete. The housings are strong enough to withstand the weight of a Jumbo as it settles on to the runway. Strobe lighting is used at some airports, and consists of sequential flashes which very clearly point the approaching pilot to the runway. On a pitch black night a runway can give the appearance of pointing into the sky. Without some other reference it is sometimes difficult to guess the angle between the runway and the approaching aircraft. A clever lighting device called VASI (Visual Approach Slope Indicator) helps pilots to approach at the correct angle. Several sets of VASIs on each side of the runway shine red and white lights at approaching aircraft. The lights are so arranged that when the pilot is set on the correct angle of descent red lights can be seen on top of white lights. If he were too high, only white lights would be seen, if too low, the red lights alone would show. Once on the ground it may be difficult to find the way to the terminal. Some airports are very large indeed and lights are necessary to guide aircraft to their stands. The taxiways are edged in blue and often have green centre lights which can be controlled from the Tower so that the pilot need be in no doubt as to which turning to take.

From early days the Meteorological office and traffic control have worked closely together. When planning a flight, pilots have always had to take the weather into consideration, and although modern jet airliners fly at high altitudes, meteorological information is still important. Various methods of gathering weather information are used, from the well-tried free balloon which carries instruments to great heights to satellites from which photographs of Earth are trans-

mitted. Data from many sources are fed into a computer which provides tabulated information for pilots and operations offices. The maps produced by the Met. offices are in use throughout the world and therefore can be understood by all nationalities. Weather data are produced in a code which, like Airimp and other international codes, is clear to all those who work with them. Although many airliners fly 'above the weather' certain hazards must be avoided if possible. The weather men can warn pilots of the presence of thunderstorms or conditions in which clear air turbulence (CAT) may be encountered. CAT can, at the very least, cause discomfort to passengers and sometimes make life difficult for the crew on the flight deck. A calm flight can suddenly become very rough, and a pilot's training includes the action to be taken when encountering CAT.

Somewhere on most major airports there is a flight training section where aircrews undergo regular checks. Flight simulators have been developed to such a degree that much of a pilot's training can take place safely on the ground. In the early years of the jet age several airliners were lost in training accidents but now simulators allow mistakes to be made without disastrous consequences. Modelled exactly on the flight deck of the airliner which it is intended to represent, the flight simulator provides an astonishing degree of

Major airports must keep snow-ploughs ready to deal with ice and snow.

realism. The instruments are driven by a computer responding to the action of the pilot. The instructor sits at a control panel from which he can introduce all sorts of problems for the pilot such as a cabin fire, engine failure, even a collapsed undercarriage. All these situations are experienced on the flight deck as if they were the real thing; the noise of the engines, the movement of the aircraft and smoke in the cockpit. Looking through the windscreen the pilots can see 'airports' and the 'surrounding countryside', usually represented by one of two methods. The earliest used a miniature landscape model and a camera fixed to a gantry. As the simulator 'flew' over the fields and towns the camera traced the flight path, throwing a picture on to a screen in front of the cockpit. A more modern system uses a computer-generated image (CGI) which consists of a television screen on which a variety of pictures can be projected:. a South African Airways Airbus is making an approach to Louis Botha airport at Durban. The night is crystal clear and the lights of the port and city soon appear under the nose, the Indian Ocean a dark shadow to the right. The flaps are lowered and as the pilot opens the throttle a little to counteract the additional drag, the growl of the two General Electric CF-6 engines can be heard behind us, the acceleration being felt as a gentle nudge in the back. The approach and runway lights come into view and moments later we make a gentle touch-down. As the runway lights flash by, however, there is an alarming crunch and we swerve wildly from side to side until

Inflatable escape slide.

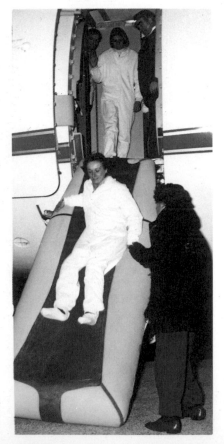

finally we come to a halt tilted steeply to the left – an undercarriage leg has collapsed! A touch of a button, however, and all is well again and the 'Airbus' is soon making another approach, this time to Port Elizabeth where patches of cloud obscure the city lights far below. Such exercises can be repeated as often as the instructor feels necessary. Experienced captains as well as young co-pilots have to undergo this type of training on a regular basis and such is the realism of simulator flying that it is every bit as demanding as the real thing. Much of the training is devoted to the take-off and landing from airports served by the airline. The CGI system not only allows several airports to be stored in the computer's memory but infinite variations in weather can be introduced too. Clear skies, 'cotton wool' cumulus cloud or a veil of mist can be conjured up to provide many different weather conditions for the pilot to encounter. A touch of another button and suddenly the pilot is in turbulent air, the simulator with its six axes motion system providing an uncomfortable degree of realism.

Flight engineers as well as pilots receive training on simulators although, of course, some training is carried out on real aircraft. For about a tenth of normal flying costs, aircrew can be given six-monthly checks on a simulator. Emergency procedures can be thoroughly learned so that the crews will react with confidence in the event of a real emergency.

Cabin crews, too, have their own simulator in the form of a mock-up. This is a reproduction of an airliner cabin in which meals can be served and instruction given. Emergency practice is not limited to the flight deck for the cabin crews too must know how to react should some-thing go wrong. As a matter of routine, the cabin crew regularly prepare for an emergency which will probably never happen. A forced landing on the sea, for example; a rapid exit down the escape chute followed by the inflation and control of the dinghies keeps the crew ready to deal with emergencies whenever they should arise.

Cabin crews must regularly undertake emergency drills including survival at sea.

Both the mock-ups and the simulators are sometimes hired out to other airlines. Airline running costs are high and by sharing facilities, significant economies can be made. This sharing extends into other fields – aircraft and engine maintenance, for example. Often airlines form 'clubs' in which training and maintenance tasks are shared. It will come as no surprise to learn that computers play an important role in aircraft maintenance. The records

of flight hours and engine running time and spare part inventories are stored in a computer. It is quite common for more than 200,000 items to be recorded in the computer, stock levels and location being available at the touch of a button. Some spares items are very expensive and once again a sharing system between airlines helps to keep costs down. Spare engines are a typical example. If an aircraft suffers an engine failure it may be

Airliners like this Boeing 747SP of South African Airways (below) are complex and require careful attention from highly trained engineers. A well-trained engineer will quickly put right a minor malfunction.

necessary to make an exchange. At many major airports the airlines have a 'pool' arrangement whereby one may draw on the spare engines of another.

We have seen that the present-day airliner is a highly complex piece of machinery. Many major airports are also the main base for the national airline. As the hub of the airline's network, the airport is the natural location for a maintenance centre; most aircraft in the fleet will spend some time there. In planning the rotation of an aircraft (the daily flight routine) an airline's planners will allow time for daily maintenance as well as for major servicing. 'On condition' maintenance helps to keep airliners ready for work at all times. Experience has shown that various components have an allotted safe life. The mechanics know that these parts can be left to work for so many hours and when their time is up

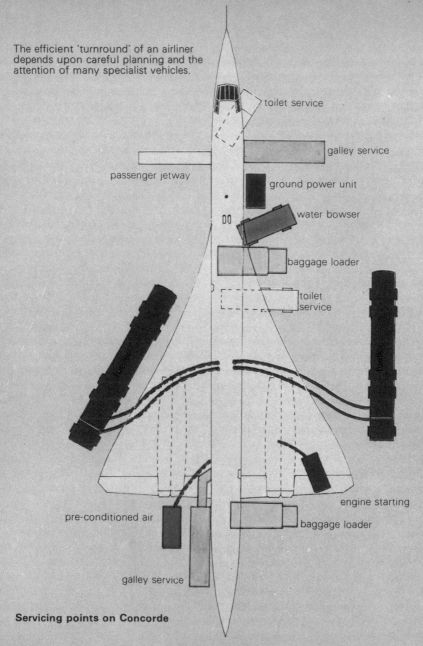

The efficient 'turnround' of an airliner depends upon careful planning and the attention of many specialist vehicles.

toilet service

galley service

passenger jetway

ground power unit

water bowser

baggage loader

toilet service

fuellers

fuellers

engine starting

pre-conditioned air

baggage loader

galley service

Servicing points on Concorde

they are simply removed and replaced by new parts. Every 10,000 flying hours or so – that means every 3 or 4 years – an airliner will undergo a major overhaul. It is stripped down and thoroughly inspected. The instruments are removed, engines are taken off, the hydraulic system is checked – no component however small, is left untested. After two or three weeks the airliner is put together again and after repainting it emerges as good as new, ready for several more years of regular work.

The maintenance bases can communicate with the airline's aircraft wherever they may be. Advice on minor problems can be given so that mechanics thousands of miles away may effect repairs. Should a major problem arise, the company's radio frequency can be used to arrange for a speedy solution. A big Rolls Royce RB211 turbo-fan can be broken down into a manageable size so that it can be loaded on to an aircraft and flown to replace another engine. Expert teams of mechanics will fly out with the spare engine to help with the exchange. They will work at any time of the day – through the night if necessary – in order to get the airliner back in the air as soon as possible.

The complexity of an airliner is reflected in the complexity of the methods of inspection in the maintenance centre. Electronic workshops, laboratories and much specialised equipment are used to ensure that the aircraft is healthy. As well as visually inspecting the spaghetti-like mass of cables, tubes and hoses, the engineers inspect the airframe closely. Bolts, rivets, screws, nuts and catches are checked and the skin is tested for cracks. Eddy-current measuring devices will spot tiny cracks which cannot be seen by the naked eye. Sometimes a penetrating dye is used to check a component; any crack will soon be shown by the searching liquid. Many parts of the aircraft are inaccessible and therefore difficult to inspect. X-ray and gamma-ray equipment is used to determine the state of metal in parts of the aircraft which cannot be seen. Boroscope probes are used to inspect the inside of a jet engine to make certain that the turbine blades are in good condition. Quite apart from the all-important safety aspect, the good condition of an airliner is important from a cost point of view too. A dent or an ill-fitting hatch can cause sufficient extra drag to make a difference to the fuel bill. Airlines have found it worthwhile to pay particular attention to the outer surfaces of their aircraft. 'Planes which are regularly washed down and kept in top condition use less fuel than dirty, battered machines. In all the aspects of running an airline, safety must always take pride of place – an airline's maintenance base therefore plays a key part in the day-to-day operations.

In the 1930s, passengers were served with cucumber sandwiches and tea. More substantial meals were taken on the ground at one of the many stops en route. Few passengers today would be prepared to spend a few days travelling to India even if nights were spent in a comfortable hotel. Airline catering, like many other aspects of modern air travel, has changed over the past 50 years. Today large numbers of passengers must be given something more substantial than cucumber sandwiches. Using considerable ingenuity, airlines supply a complete meal on a tray, several courses being fitted together to ease the task for the steward or stewardess. The food is prepared in large kitchens where experienced staff duplicate dishes by the hundred. Coloured catalogues show the caterers just what the meal should look like. To be appetising, a meal must look attractive, so careful attention is given to

Every effort is made to provide appetising meals for economy class (*above*) and first-class (*right*) passengers.
Inset Early British Airways catering.

the appearance of the food. The quantity or weight of each portion is set out in catalogues for there is no room for guess-work. Only the meals for first-class passengers are specially prepared on board the aircraft. The economy class passengers are served meals which have been pre-cooked and frozen. Although it is difficult, airlines try to provide first class passengers with meals of a standard one would expect of a first class hotel. The hors d'oeuvre is served from a trolley and special dishes are cooked in the first class galley. Fresh fruit, a selection of cheeses, cigars and liqueurs add to the air of luxury for the first class passengers. Special meals can usually be provided by the airline's kitchens although sometimes the services of another carrier may be used if a Moslem or kosher meal is required. Baby foods and other special refreshments are supplied by the kitchens, which are notified by the airline's Operations office of any special requests. (Our old friend the computer will, of course, make a note of such requirements when the booking is made.) The large airlines prepare millions of meals each year and often supply smaller airlines which do not have catering facilities of their own. To keep costs to a minimum, much of the catering equipment is used only once; plastic cutlery and cups are thrown away, and the luxury of steel knives and forks, china and glassware is usually reserved for first class passengers.

Although international air travel has enabled millions of people to move around the world with ease, it has also stimulated the movement of some unwelcome travellers. Countries which have all but eliminated some diseases have found that they have been re-introduced by air travel. Tuberculosis, malaria, even leprosy, have been picked up by businessmen or tourists and taken to countries which are free of such diseases. Airport medical centres are often called upon to advise on the condition of a sick passenger or provide vaccinations for those who may have had contact with a typhoid carrier. Doctors and nurses are on hand to aid those who have had an accident or suffered a heart attack, and the medical centre has an operating theatre for emergency cases. At the larger airports a dentist is also on hand to fix an aching tooth.

Below A first-aid demonstration.

Like any city, a big airport has its fair share of crime and consequently a permanent police force is necessary. Valuable cargo and rich passengers are targets for the skilled criminal or the petty thief – both provide the police with constant problems. It is, alas, all too easy for the dishonest baggage handler to 'drop' a suitcase so that it bursts open to reveal its contents. Sometimes gold or diamonds have been the target of armed robbers. To cloak a valuable cargo in secrecy a gold shipment may be described as, for example, razor blades, and, of course, the majority of shipments do reach their destination safely. On a more mundane level, road traffic at an airport can cause as much of a problem as it does in a city. Certainly police at airports have enough to keep them fully occupied throughout their duty.

TV monitors are used to keep a close eye on road traffic at Heathrow.

Another service which all airports maintain is fortunately rarely used – the fire department. Although frequently put on alert, the fire services only occasionally have to practise their skills. A burning airliner can be destroyed in a few minutes which is why fire services must be kept in constant practice. The spearhead of the rescue services is the rapid intervention vehicle (RIV). Based on a small vehicle such as a Range Rover, the RIV is capable of high speeds over rough terrain and can deliver foam on to a burning wreck before the arrival of the airfield crash tender. Capable of being operated by one man, a modern crash tender can deliver thousands of gallons of water and foam from a turret on the roof of the vehicle. The firemen are trained to cut their way into a crashed aircraft and bring out the shocked passengers who will often be unable to help themselves. Some remarkable rescues have taken place from airliners which have become a total loss. The timely arrival of a fire tender can keep the flames at bay long enough for the passengers to get out. At Heathrow the fire service is put on an alert almost daily, for an engine failure or other potential hazard may result in a crash. In fact it rarely does, but the fire services are ready to move at the first sign of disaster.

Left Regular practise is necessary if fire crews are to be capable of putting out a fire quickly.

Top This powerful Chubb Pathfinder crash tender can direct foam on to a fire within seconds of its arrival at the scene of a crashed airliner.

Above Every second counts as powerful crash tenders speed to a crashed aircraft.

Air crashes are fortunately rare, but airports must be prepared for disasters. Police, hospitals and fire services in the neighbourhood of airports practise a disaster drill from time to time, just in case. Many airports are situated close to the coast. Indeed, the runway at Hong Kong extends into the harbour and the airports of Copenhagen, Nice and Genoa are right by the sea. At such airports, the rescue facilities must include speed-boats which can reach a wreck quickly. At some airports hovercraft have been added to the rescue equipment so that help can be speeded across land, water or marsh.

As a nation of animal lovers, the British would be expected to provide help to animal travellers. A great variety pass through Heathrow each year and many need the attention of the RSPCA hostel staff. As well as providing accommodation for lions, elephants, snakes and dolphins, the hostel has an operating theatre for the treatment of injured animals. Unfortunately injuries are common because animals are often transported in poor conditions. Considerable courage is sometimes necessary when the RSPCA officials are asked to recover escaped animals. Poisonous snakes, bears – all manner of dangerous creatures – have been

Below and opposite At the end of their journeys, or in transit between flights, animals are looked after by officials of the RSPCA.

Above A BOAC Avro York and some jumbos!

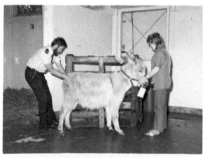

recaptured by skilled officials. It is not unknown for a frog or snake to be let loose in an airliner's cabin by a young passenger who had decided that perhaps his pet would not be welcome at home!

Getting to and from an airport has become an important aspect of air travel. It is possible to fly from Paris to London in about 40 minutes – and it will take at least that time to reach the centre of the city. A number of airports are now linked to the city by a rail or underground service. The underground station at Heathrow now carries the bulk of the passengers who used to take the bus services to London. Brussels, Frankfurt, Dusseldorf and Paris are among the airports which have rail links to the city centre, and although many have excellent motorway connections, an increasing number of passengers avoid the traffic jams by taking a train. Links between airports can be important, for many passengers flying into one will want to connect with flights leaving from another. For many years New York Airways has provided a regular service between the principal airports and to the city. With traffic through both Heathrow and Gatwick growing steadily, the British Airports Authority saw the need for a helicopter connection between the two and has been successfully operating the Air Link service for some time.

Yet another similarity between airports and cities lies in the growing number of hotels which have been built to meet the needs of passengers and aircrews. Multi-national companies hold meetings at airports because businessmen from several countries can fly into an airport, have a conference at an hotel, and depart, all within 24 hours. Precious time getting to and from the city centre can be saved by staying at an airport hotel. Passengers in transit between flights are frequent users of airport hotels and, of course, when fog descends, Jumbo-loads of passengers are glad of the opportunity to find a bed so close to the airport.

As in a city, the hustle and bustle of a busy airport can be exciting. Certainly airports receive many visitors besides those who are actually travelling.

A helicopter service provides a regular link between London's Heathrow and Gatwick airports.

At Dallas special rail-borne carriages convey passengers about the airport (*above*). A special control room (*below*) is necessary.

Into the blue

The airliner of today is a complex and very expensive piece of equipment.

To make it pay its way, much careful planning is necessary so that as much time as possible is spent in the air. Most airlines change their schedules at least twice a year so that major servicing can be carried out in the winter months. This ensures that as many aircraft as possible are available to meet the demand for flights at the peak of the summer season.

Expert planners decide on the 'rotation' of the aircraft in the airline fleet. Careful judgement is called for to satisfy the requirements of engineers, airport authorities, sales departments and many others concerned with airline operations. Like pieces of a jigsaw puzzle, the daily routine of each aircraft fits into the overall pattern. If the planners could get fourteen hours of revenue-earning flight every day from each aircraft they would be doing well; very few airliners, in fact, manage to achieve this total.

The aircrews are little concerned with all this complex planning except that they too happen to be an important element in the jigsaw because there are strict limits on the number of hours which they can fly each day. Safety demands that crew members are fit and alert at all times – so excessive working hours

for flying staff are not permitted.

About an hour before the scheduled departure of an airliner the aircrew reports for duty. The captain, co-pilots, and flight engineer all have tasks to perform. The pilots receive a briefing from the flight despatcher and they calculate the weight and plan the route for the aircraft. Previously the flight details were worked out by using graphs

and calculators. Nowadays computers take much of the tedium out of the task and complex problems can be solved in a matter of minutes, reducing the work load of the crew.

In considering the route to be flown by the aircraft, the captain has to be aware of the weather forecast and he must know the total number of passengers and the weight of cargo which has been booked. With this information to hand the crew will then be able to work out how much fuel will need to be carried. It is a matter of routine that much more fuel is loaded than is expected to be used, for the airliner must be capable of flying on to alternative airports which are selected in case the destination is closed for some reason. Perhaps sudden fog will make a landing impossible, or maybe an aircraft has become stuck on the runway; whatever the reason, an airline must be prepared for such eventualities and sufficient fuel loaded accordingly. Skillful calculations are called for because it is

An airline operations room is the centre from which the fleet of aircraft is controlled.

very wasteful to carry too much fuel on a journey. Many advanced airliners are equipped with computers which automatically adjust the throttles so that the minimum amount of fuel is consumed.

On long over-water journeys there are often a number of alternative routes which the captain may select but on many overland flights between cities there is little opportunity to alter the route. Only changes in height may be possible if more favourable weather conditions are sought.

When the pilots are satisfied about the route details, a flight plan is 'filed'. That is to say all those concerned with the flight are sent a telex copy of the details; in addition to the air traffic control authorities at the departure and arrival points, the zones through which the aircraft will fly are also informed. The flight plans for most scheduled flights are stored in a computer and activated an hour before departure.

With this part of the paperwork done, the flight crew then work out the speeds to be attained at take-off. This will depend upon the load, the height of the runway above sea-level and the temperature. The performance of an airliner will vary considerably in different temperatures and air densities, so the airline's planners must see that the best possible conditions are chosen. For example, most long distance flights into or out of Nairobi are generally scheduled to take place at night or early in the morning, to

Air and ground crews attend to the needs of passengers at all stages of a journey.

avoid the high temperatures of the midday sun. Although only a few feet above sea level, the airport at Bahrain can get very hot indeed. This sometimes reduces the payload of the Concorde from 100 passengers to 70 or so.

The flight engineer is responsible for the serviceability of the aircraft throughout the journey and keeps a watchful eye on the fuel state. Before take-off he will inspect the aircraft to make certain that all hatches are closed and the aircraft is undamaged. (It is not unknown for a truck on the tarmac to bump into an aircraft!) On board, he monitors the many instruments which indicate how the engines are performing and how much fuel is being used. It is typical of the

double-check safety system of airlines that the captain, too, inspects the aircraft externally before taking his seat on the flight deck.

The cabin crew obviously have to prepare for the new passenger load, the senior steward or purser taking a note of any important passengers who may be booked. The meals for the journey are checked and if vegetarian or other special food has been requested the cabin crew must make sure that it is on board. Children travelling alone, wheelchair passengers or others in special need will be given a helping hand by a friendly stewardess.

Whilst these routine preparations are proceeding, baggage, cargo and mail are being loaded in the belly of the aircraft. The flight despatcher is responsible for the correct balance of the load and he keeps an eagle eye on the loaders to make sure that the right holds are used. As much freight can be carried beneath the passenger cabins of a wide-body airliner as would once have been carried on an all-cargo aircraft. Containers of various shapes and sizes have been produced to carry particular types of cargo. Insulated containers can carry vegetables or such delicacies as lobster and giant prawns. Special containers fitted with racks are used to carry clothes which can be sold on arrival without the need for ironing. Small packages are loaded into other containers or 'igloos' so that the loading of the aircraft may be carried out quickly.

Pilots refer to check lists (*above and right*) several times during a flight.

loaded with the same ease as containerised cargo.

As well as the special cargo and baggage loading vehicles, the food for the passengers is brought to the aircraft in a special truck equipped with a scissors lift. This elevates the body of the truck to the required height so that the food containers can be delivered direct to the galley.

As the time for departure approaches, one by one the vehicles around the airliner leave the scene. The re-fueller, the baggage trucks and water trucks, all move to their next assignment, leaving the powerful tug which will push the airliner on to the apron when the time comes to start the engines.

As the passengers come on board, the flight deck will be the scene of pre-start-up checks – the first of many checks which will be made during the journey. As many as 225 items have to be checked before a SAS DC-9 can take off, for example. Once the captain is satisfied that all is well, the engines are started. Little more than a whine or a growl can be heard from the cockpit and even passengers in the part of the cabin closest to the engines will not find the noise too intrusive. Even before the engines are started, the co-pilot will call for flight clearance and the air traffic controller will give clear instructions for the start of the journey. The crew will be told to which height they must climb and the courses to steer as the airliner wings its way to its first waypoint.

Some special cargo has to be handled carefully; live tropical fish, radio-active materials and some awkwardly-shaped pieces of machinery, for instance. These may have to be loaded with special equipment or put into heated or insulated parts of the aircraft. Special attention must be paid to hazardous cargo – inflammable or corrosive substances or radio-active materials.

On some aircraft passengers' baggage is loaded directly into the hold, care being taken to separate cases which are destined for different airports. Mobile conveyor belts aid the baggage loaders although the trend is towards putting baggage into containers so that it can be

COCKPIT PREPARATION CHECKLIST (PILOT TO RESPOND)

```
Oxygen Masks . . . . . . . . . . . . . . . . . CHECKED
ENG FIRE Handle and AGT LO Lts . . . . . STOWED/OFF
HYD FLT CONTROL Lts . . . . . . . . . . . . . . . . OFF
FLAP LIMIT Sel . . . . . . . . . . . . . . . . . . . AUTO
ELEV FEEL Sel . . . . . . . . . . . . . . . . . . . AUTO
ADG Sw . . . . . . . . . . . . . . . . . . . . . . . . HYD
YAW DAMP Sws . . . . . . . . . . . . . . CHECKED/ON
ANTI-SKID Sws . . . . . . . . . . . . . . CHECKED/OFF
MSU/CDU . . . . . . . . . . . . . . . . . CHECKED/SET
COMPASS Sw . . . . . . . SLAVED/MDG X-CHECK
VOR and INS Sels . . . . . . . . . . . . . . . . . NORM
F/D CMD and CADC Sels . . . . . . . . . . . . NORM
ENG Start Panel . . . . . . . . . . . . . . . . CHECKED
EMER PWR Sw . . . . . . . . . . . . . . . . . . . . OFF
EMER Lts . . . . . . . . . . . . . . . . CHECKED/ARM
NO SMOKE and SEAT BELTS Sws . . . . . . . . . ON
PA . . . . . . . . . . . . . . . . . . . . . . . . CHECKED
GPWS . . . . . . . . . . . . . . . CHECKED/NORMAL
STALL and MAX SPD WARN Sys . . . . . . CHECKED
SPD CONT . . . . . . . . . . . . . . . . . . CHECKED
WINDSHLD ANTI-ICE/DEFOG Sels . . . . OFF/ON
Pitot Heat . . . . . . . . . . . . . . . . CHECKED/ON
ENG ANTI-ICE Sels . . . . . . . . . . . . . . . . . OFF
Lights . . . . . . . . . . . . . . . . . . . . . . AS REQ'D
AP Levers . . . . . . . . . . . . . . . . CHECKED/OFF
Stby Horizon . . . . . . . . . . . . . . . . . . . ERECT
ENG Instrs . . . . . . . . . . . . . . . . . . CHECKED
FLAP/SLAT Pos Ind . . . . . . . . . . . . . CHECKED
SURF POS Ind . . . . . . . . . . . . . . . . CHECKED
GEAR . . . . . . . . . . . . . . . . . DOWN/3 GREEN
LONG TRIM . . . . . . . . . . . . . . . . . CHECKED
SPOILERS . . . . . . . . . . . . . . . . . RETRACTED
WARNING HORN . . . . . . . . . . . . . . CHECKED
FLAP/SLAT Handles . . . . . . . . . . . . . UP/RET
Rudder and AIL Trim . . . . . . . . . CHECK/ZERO
ADG RELEASE Handle . . . . . . . . . . . SAFETIED
Radar . . . . . . . . . . . . . . . . . . . . . . . . . STBY
Flight Instrs . . . . . . . . . . . . . . . . . CHECKED
Radio NAV . . . . . . . . . . . . . . . . . . CHECKED
Altimeters . . . . . . . . . . . . . . . . . . CHECKED
```

TAXI CHECKLIST (F/E TO CHALLENGE TAXI THRU PARKING/SHUTDOWN)

```
Altimeters . . . . . (C-F) . . . . QNH SET/X-CHECKED
                                       STANDBY 1013
FLAPS . . . . . . . . . (F) . . . . . . . . . . DEGREES
ANTI-SKID . . . . . . . (F) . . . . . . . . . . . ARMED
Flight Controls . . . . (F) . . . . . . . . . CHECKED
Fuel Panel . . . . . . . (E) . . . . . . . . SET FOR T.O.
APU . . . . . . . . . . . (E) . . . . . . . . . AS REQ'D
Thrust Computer . . . . (F-E). . . . . . SET FOR T.O.
Harness and Seats . . . (C-F-E) . . . . SECURE/OFF
Flight Instrs . . . . . . (C-F). . . . . . . . CHECKED
CDU . . . . . . . . . . . (C-F). . . . . . . . CHECKED
Crew Briefing . . . . . (C-F-E). . . . . UNDERSTOOD
```

TAKEOFF CHECKLIST

```
HYD Panel . . . . . . . . (E) . . . . CHECKED/ARMED
ALT Select . . . . . . . . (P) . . . . . . . . . SET . . . FT
FLAPS/SLATS . . . . . . (C-F) . . . . QUADRANT AND
                                       GAGES CHECKED
                                    _____ DEGREES T.O.
                                          LIGHT ON
Cabin Report . . . . . . (C) . . . . . . . . . RECEIVED
PA . . . . . . . . . . . . . (C) . . . . . . . . COMPLETE
ANTI-ICING . . . . . . . (P-E) . . . . . . . AS REQ'D
Spoiler Handle . . . . . (C) . . . . . . . . . . ARMED
Transponder . . . . . . (P) . . . . . . . . . . . . . ON
Annunciator Lights . . (P-E) . . . . . . . . CHECKED
Pneumatics . . . . . . . (E) . . . . . . . . . AS REQ'D
ENG IGNITION Sel . . . (E). . . . . . CONT A OR B
External Lights . . . . (P) . . . . . . . . . . . . . ON
Ready for T.O. . . . . . (A) . . . . . . . . . . . READY
```

CLIMB CHECKLIST

```
EXT Lights . . . . . . . . (P). . . . . . . . . AS REQ'D
GEAR . . . . . . . . . . . (P). . . . . UP/LIGHTS OUT
FLAP/SLATS . . . . . . . (P). . . . . . . . . . UP/RET
Spoilers . . . . . . . . . (C). . . . . . . . DISARMED
ENG IGNITION Sel . . . (P). . . . . . . . . AS REQ'D
NO SMOKE/SEAT BELTS Sws (P). . . . . . AS REQ'D
Altimeters . . . . . . . . (C-F). QNH SET/X-CHECKED
Pressurization . . . . . . (E). . . . . . . . . CHECKED
Altimeters at Transition (C-F). . . . . . STANDARD
                                       SET/X-CHECKED
```

PRE-DEPARTURE CHECKLIST (F/E TO RESPOND)

```
APU and Eng Fire Det Sys . . . . . . . . . . CHECKED
CAB PRESS MAN/AUTO . . . . . . . . . . . . . AUTO
CAB OUTFLOW VALVE Pos . . . . . . . . . . . OPEN
HYD Sys . . . . . . . . . . . TEMPS NORMAL MOTOR
                             AND AUX PUMPS OFF
Elec Sys and GALLEY Pwr . . . . . . . . . . . NORMAL
Fuel Panel . . . . . . . . . . . . . . . . . . . . . . SET
Manifold Fail Lts . . . . . . . . . . . . . . . CHECKED
Pneu and Air Cond . . . . . . . . . . . . . . . NORMAL
Cargo Compt Temp . . . . . . . . . . . . . . CHECKED
Water/Qty/Press. . . . . . . . CHECK/WHITE BAND
O2 Qty/Press. . . . . . . . . . . CHECK/WHITE BAND
Oxy Mask Eject Sw . . . . . . . . NORMAL/GUARDED
Cabin Press. . . . . . . . . . . . . . . CHECKED/SET
Engine Vibration Sys . . . . . . . CHECKED AND SET
Engine Instrs . . . . . . . . . . . . . . . . . CHECKED
FLIGHT RECORDER . . . . . . . . . . . . . . . . . SET
Oxy Mask . . . . . . . . . . . . . . . . . . . CHECKED
```

PRE-DEPARTURE CHECKLIST (PILOT TO CHALLENGE)

```
FD Sws . . . . . . . . . . . (P) . . . . . . . . . . . OFF
ATS Levers . . . . . . . . (P) . . . . . . . . . . . OFF
AP Levers . . . . . . . . . (P) . . . . . . . . . . . OFF
NAV Radios/HSI Sw . . . (C-F) . . . . . . . . . . SET
INS . . . . . . . . . . . . . (C-F) . . . . SET AS REQ'D
Brakes . . . . . . . . . . . (P) . . . . . . . . . PARKED
FUEL Levers . . . . . . . (P) . . . . . . . . . . . OFF
Fuel Qty . . . . . . . . . . (C-E) . . . . . . . . . . . LB
Technical Logs and
  Loadsheet . . . . . . . (C-E) . . . . . . ON BOARD
GEAR Pins and Pitot Covers (E) . . . . . ON BOARD
T.O. Data . . . . . . . . . (C-F) . . . . CHECKED/SET
LONG TRIM . . . . . . . . (C-F) . . . . . . . . . . SET
Windows . . . . . . . . . . (C-F). OVERCENTER/LOCKED
MSU . . . . . . . . . . . . . (C-F) . . . . . . . . . NAV
START CLEARANCE . . . (P) . . . . . . . RECEIVED
```

DESCENT CHECKLIST

```
Safety Height . . . . . . . (C-F) . . . . . . CHECKED
Altimeters . . . . . . . . . (C-F) . . . . SET/X-CHECKED
Pressurization . . . . . . . (E) . . . . . . . . . . . SET
Landing Data . . . . . . . (F-E) . . . . . . . CHECKED
Hydraulic Pumps . . . . . . . . . . . . . . . ALL ON
Approach Review and
  Landing Briefing . . . . (C) . . . . . . . . COMPLETE
```

APPROACH CHECKLIST

```
NO SMOKE/SEAT BELTS Sws (C) . . . . . . AUTO/ON
Shoulder Harness/Seats . . (A) . . . . . . SECURE/OFF
ANTI-ICE Sys . . . . . . . . (F) . . . . . . . AS REQ'D
NAV Radios/HSI Sw . . . . (A) . . . . . . . . SET/IA
Thrust Computer . . . . . . (E) . . . . . . . . SET/IA
Fuel Panel . . . . . . . . . . (E) . . . . . . . . . . SET
Altimeters . . . . . . . . . . (A) . . . PASSING TRANSITION
                                         LEVEL QNH
                                         SET/X-CHECK
```

LANDING CHECKLIST

```
Altimeters . . . . . . . . (C-F) . . CAPT TO QFE X-CHECK
                                    HEIGHT DIFF. BOTH SET
                                    TO QFE FOR LANDING
Critical Height . . . . . . (C-F) . . . . . . . SET ON
                                     RADIO ALTIMETERS
Gear . . . . . . . . . . . . . (A) . . . . DOWN 3 GREEN
BRAKE Press. . . . . . . . (P) . . . . . . . . CHECKED
ANTI-SKID . . . . . . . . . (P) . . . . . CHECKED/ARMED
Spoiler Handle . . . . . . (P) . . . . . . . . . ARMED
FLAPS/SLATS . . . . . . . (P) . . . . . . DEGREES/LAND
ENG IGNITION Sel . . . . (E). . . . . . CONT A OR B
Hydraulic Panel . . . . . (P) . . . . . . . . CHECKED
Annunciator Lights . . . (P-E) . . . . . . . CHECKED
External Lights . . . . . . (P) . . . . . . . . . . . ON
Auto Pilot/Throttles . . . (P) . . . . . . . . . . OFF
```

PRE-START CHECKLIST (PILOT TO CHALLENGE)

```
Beacon Lt . . . . . . . . . . (P). . . . . . . . . . . ON
FUEL Pumps . . . . . . . . (E). . . . . . . SET 1-2-1
Ground Crew Report . . . (E). . . . CLEAR TO START
Doors . . . . . . . . . . . . . (C). . . . . . . . . . . ARM
Door W/L . . . . . . . . . . (E). . . . . . . . . . . OUT
CARGO DOORS. . . . . . . (E). . . . . PHYSICALLY
                                       CHECKED SECURE
Air Cond PACKS . . . . . . (E). . . . . . . . ALL OFF
ENG IGNITION Sel . . . . (P). . . . . START A OR B
Pneu Press. . . . . . . . . . . . . . . . . . . . . . . LB
```

AFTER START CHECKLIST (PILOT TO CHALLENGE)

```
Disconnect (If Required)

ENG IGNITION Sel . . . . . (P). . . . . . . . . . . OFF
ENG ANTI-ICE . . . . . . . (P). . . . . . . . AS REQ'D
Electrics . . . . . . . . . . . (E). . . . . . . . . . . SET
Pneu and Air Cond . . . . (E). . . . . . NORM/AUTO
Hand Signals . . . . . . . . (C). . . . . . . . . CLEAR
Push-Back Taxi Clrnc . . . (C). . . . . . . RECEIVED

                    NOTE
   Repeat After Start Check after delayed Engine 2 Start.
```

AFTER LANDING CHECKLIST

```
EXT Lights . . . . . . . . . . (F) . . . . . . AS REQ'D
Radar and Transponder . . (F) . . . . . . OFF/STBY
FLAPS/SLATS . . . . . . . . (F) . . . . . . . UP/RET
Spoiler . . . . . . . . . . . . (F) . . . . . . DISARMED
BRAKE Pressure . . . . . . (F) . . . CHECKED MONITOR
APU . . . . . . . . . . . . . . (F) . . . . . . AS REQ'D
ENG IGNITION Sel . . . . . (F) . . . . . . . . . . OFF
ANTI-ICE . . . . . . . . . . . (F-E) . . . . . . . . . OFF
ANTI-SKID . . . . . . . . . . (F) . . . . . . . . . . . OFF
MOTOR PUMP Sws . . . . . (E) . . . . . . AS REQ'D
```

PARKING SHUTDOWN CHECKLIST

```
                    NOTE
Items down to black line to be completed on transit. All items to
be completed with crew change.

Doors . . . . . . . . . . . . . . . . (C). . . . DISARMED
PARK Brake . . . . . . . . . . . . . (C). . . . . PARKED
FUEL Levers . . . . . . . . . . . . (C). . . . . . . OFF
EXT Lights and BEACON . . . . . (F). . . . AS REQ'D
                                             OFF
Hyd, Elec, Fuel, Pneu and
  Air Cond . . . . . . . . . . . . . (E). . . . . . . SET
INS . . . . . . . . . . . . . . . . . . (E). . . . AS REQ'D
CHOCKS/Park Brakes . . . (C) . . . . . . . OFF

WINDSHLD ANTI-ICE and
  DEFOG Sws . . . . . . . . . . . (F). . . . . . . . OFF
PITOT Ht . . . . . . . . . . . . . . . (F). . . . . . . OFF
EMER LT . . . . . . . . . . . . . . . (E). . . . . . . OFF
INS . . . . . . . . . . . . . . . . . . (C-F). . . . . . . OFF
APU . . . . . . . . . . . . . . . . . . (E). . . . . . . OFF
BAT Sw . . . . . . . . . . . . . . . . (E). . . . AS REQ'D
```

Morse code

A	.—	S	...
B	—...	T	—
C	—.—.	U	..—
D	—..	V	...—
E	.	W	.——
F	..—.	X	—..—
G	——.	Y	—.——
H	....	Z	——..
I	..	1	.————
J	.———	2	..———
K	—.—	3	...——
L	.—..	4	....—
M	——	5	.....
N	—.	6	—....
O	———	7	——...
P	.——.	8	———..
Q	——.—	9	————.
R	.—.	0	—————
Full stop			.—.—.—
Semicolon			—.—.—.
Comma			——..——
Colon			———...
Interrogation			..——..
Apostrophe			.————.
Hyphen			—....—
Bracket			—.——.—
Inverted commas			.—..—.
Underline			..——.—
Double dash			—...—
Distress signal (S.O.S.)			...———...
Attention signal			—.—.—
Invitation to transmit			—.—
Wait			.—...
Break			—...—.—
Understood			...—.
Error			....
Received			.—.
Position report			—.—.
End of message			.—.—.
Finish of transmission			...—.—

The International Phonetic Alphabet

A	N
Alfa	November
B	O
Bravo	Oscar
C	P
Charlie	Papa
D	Q
Delta	Quebec
E	R
Echo	Romeo
F	S
Foxtrot	Sierra
G	T
Golf	Tango
H	U
Hotel	Uniform
I	V
India	Victor
J	W
Juliett	Whiskey
K	X
Kilo	X-ray
L	Y
Lima	Yankee
M	Z
Mike	Zulu

Ways to memorise morse

Dots		Dashes	
.	E	—	T
..	I	——	M
...	S	———	O
....	H	(no four dashes)	
.....	5	—————	Zero

Opposites

A	.—	N	—.
U	..—	D	—..
R	.—.	K	—.—
V	...—	B	—...
W	.——	G	——.
F	..—.	L	.—..
P	.——.	X	—..—

All pilots use the international phonetic alphabet, and many are at least familiar with the Morse Code.

Over the years a radio jargon has evolved which is understood internationally. As America has been the pioneer in much of air transport it is not surprising that English has become generally accepted as the international aviation language. A Belgian Sabena captain flying to Madrid or a KLM crew in Bangkok will find mutual understanding through the use of English – although it is a rather special English. By using the same phrases in all parts of the world, misunderstandings can be avoided. *Caledonian 884 is cleared standard Seaford one-seven departure to Charles de Gaulle. Climb to flight level two-one-zero on the Seaford three-five-zero radial and squawk Alpha two-zero-* *zero-nine* may sound gibberish to the casual listener but for the British Caledonian crew taking a BAC One-Eleven from Gatwick to Paris/ Charles de Gaulle the message is clear. It is an example of the radio 'shorthand' which enables complex messages to be passed quickly and clearly. In this case, air traffic control is telling the pilots that a particular route laid down in a departure manual (standard Seaford one-seven) must be taken, followed by a climb to 21,000 feet. On take-off the transponder should signal 'A2009' so that the aircraft can be identified on the radar screens of the controllers, and a further clearance can be issued.

With clearance granted, the Ground Movement Planner gives permission for the engines to be started and a powerful tug pushes the airliner back so that it can begin to taxi to the runway. There is often a queue of airliners waiting to take off and slowly the great airliner edges forward until finally it is time to line up on the runway. Take-off permission given, the co-pilot firmly opens the throttles while the captain steers the nosewheel by a tiller. Back in the cabin the passengers can feel the surge of power and a sudden increase in engine noise. At first the aircraft seems to move so slowly that some may wonder how it could possibly get into the air. Nevertheless, the great craft gathers pace and as the take-off speed is neared the co-pilot calls out airspeed: 'One-thirty, one-forty, V-one', and finally 'V-R', as the captain pulls on the control column to nose the aircraft into the air. During this critical phase of the journey the flight engineer is not idle but has swung his seat between the pilots to aid the pilot as he pushes the throttles open.

You will remember that one of the tasks of the pilots when preparing for the flight was to calculate the speeds for take-off. V-1 is the decision speed by which the captain must choose between continuing with the take-off run or applying the brakes if he considers that there is something wrong. V-R or Rotate is the precise speed at which the take-off is made, though after V-1 the aircraft cannot be stopped. With the nose lifted into the air, the airliner climbs majestically away. V-2 is the minimum speed at which the aircraft makes its climb out of the airport area.

In the United States 'queues' to take off are quite common at the larger airports.

First-time passengers may feel a little nervous about some unusual noises during the first moments of a flight. For example, when the throttles are fully opened for take-off, what had been a distant whine suddenly turns into a deep-throated roar. The almost noiseless hiss of the cabin air pressurization stops during the initial climb but returns within a matter of minutes. When it seems that the aircraft has only just climbed a few thousand feet, the throttles are suddenly pulled back and the noise of the engines dies to a whine again. Engine failure? An emergency perhaps? No, it is simply part of the routine to minimize the aircraft noise which has to be endured by those living near airports. Many modern airliners are significantly quieter than earlier jets – despite the fact that the jumbo-sized aircraft are much bigger than first-generation types. Nevertheless, the age of the silent aircraft is not yet with us and all aircraft using major airports are required to use noise abatement techniques – hence the sudden reduction in noise only minutes after take-off.

More noises may arouse the curiosity of passengers seated comfortably in the cabin; a groan followed by a thump signifies that the hydraulic system has retracted the undercarriage and more groans will accompany the gradual retraction of the flaps. As the various high-lift devices are tucked into the wing it takes on its most efficient shape for high speed and – with the permission of the air traffic controller – the airliner will begin its climb to cruising altitude. Although the pressurization system will maintain the cabin at a comfortable level, some passengers may experience some discomfort during the climb – especially those suffering from colds. Sucking a sweet, yawning or swallowing can help to clear any 'popping' ears.

As the passengers settle down to enjoy the flight, the cabin crew spring into action, erecting stowable trolleys and preparing to serve the meals. Some of the larger airliners feature an under-floor galley in which the stewards or stewardesses can prepare the meals. As 345 passengers wing their way to a Mediterranean holiday in a Laker Airways DC-10, meals are heated and then sent up in lifts to be distributed from trolleys. High speed microwave ovens quickly heat succulent steaks which have been prepared in kitchens some hours before and kept frozen until needed.

While the cabin crew is attending to the needs of the passengers, those on the flight deck are settling on to the course outlined in the flight plan. A series of 'way-points' plots the course of the flight to the destination. In the crowded skies of Europe or America it is not possible to fly direct from A to B, because uncontrolled air traffic would be too dangerous. Instead, great airways in the sky link navigation beacons. As important to a pilot as a lighthouse to a ship's captain, the VOR beacons 'light' the way of the airliners flying high above. Very High Frequency Omni-directional Range is the full title of these beacons. (Hardly surprising that the term VOR is preferred!) An instrument on the flight deck indicates the direction of the next VOR but another instrument called the DME (Distance Measuring Equipment) will indicate precisely how far it is to the next beacon by sending an interrogation signal and measuring the reply. Incredibly accurate devices are used nowadays to navigate airliners over great distances. Using gyroscopes and accelerometers the INS (Inertial Navigation System) senses every movement of the aircraft and can relate it to the exact position of the airliner on take-off. The waypoints over which the aircraft will fly can be 'punched in' to the system and as the journey progresses the autopilot will, at the command of the pilot, gently bring the aircraft on to a new direction.

Left The VOR needles point to the transmitters. *Right* the DME indicators show the distance from the transmitters.

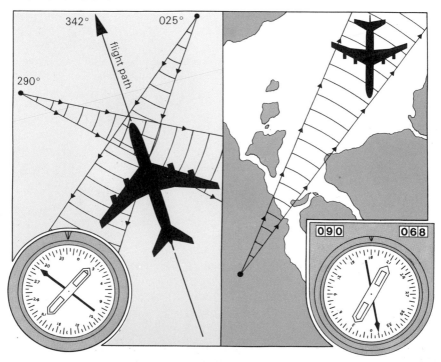

The touch of a button will make the autopilot move the aircraft on to a different heading without the pilot touching the control column at all.

Omega is another navigational system of great accuracy. Several radio stations dotted about the world transmit very long wave radio signals at regular intervals – three pulses, each on a different frequency, are sent out every ten seconds. A computer on board the aircraft calculates its exact position after analysing the signals. Small wonder that navigators have long ceased to be part of the flight deck crew of a modern airliner.

It may be wondered if the crew spend the long hours of flight reading a book or playing cards. Although there are many aids on board an airliner to ease the task of air crews, safety demands that they remain alert and ready to deal with any eventuality. The flight engineer, for example, sits before an instrument panel and monitors the electric power, air conditioning, pressurization, oxygen and fuel flow. In addition, the engine exhaust pres-

Air traffic control (ATC) keep airliners safely separated, with the help of computers.

sure, the RPM of the high and low pressure compressors and the exhaust temperature are indicated on the flight engineer's panel. He keeps a diary of the flight, noting any faults which arise during the journey As the flight engineer also helps during take-off and landing, you can see that he is kept busy enough! Of course, not all aircraft carry a flight engineer, but all the tasks performed by him must be carried out by a member of the flight crew.

The co-pilot too has a regular task to perform: as the aircraft

passes from one control zone to another he maintains radio contact with the controllers far below. Remember that the flight plan has been telexed to all points along the way and therefore the airliner is expected at a pre-determined time. Some delays can occur, however, and a junction can become too busy for safety. In such cases an airliner may be asked to alter course or perhaps fly a complete circle while the 'traffic jam' is dispersed. The pilots, too, have their instruments to monitor; once in a while an auto-pilot will 'run away' and fail to keep the aircraft on the correct course. Weather radar can look ahead for 240 kilometres and if a storm is indicated the pilots may request permission from the controllers to alter course. Often such minor course changes go unnoticed by the passengers for a gentle movement of the controls can barely be detected by those enjoying a good book or a meal.

Even if evading action is not necessary, the progress of the flight must be advised regularly to the controllers so that a clear picture of the air traffic is kept below on the radar screens. Every airliner carries a transponder which can transmit a signal to the ATC. The signal carries an identification code which shows on the controller's radar screen thus ensuring that he knows which 'blip' belongs to whom, and can also transmit the height at which the aircraft is to fly.

Radar aids

Radar plays a vital role in plotting the position of airliners, detecting far-off storms and even spotting flocks of geese. Precision approach radar, P.A.R., can provide approach path and height information to the controller.

Secondary radar (*above right*), not only gives the controller the aircraft position but also the height and callsign, thanks to signals transmitted by the aircraft.

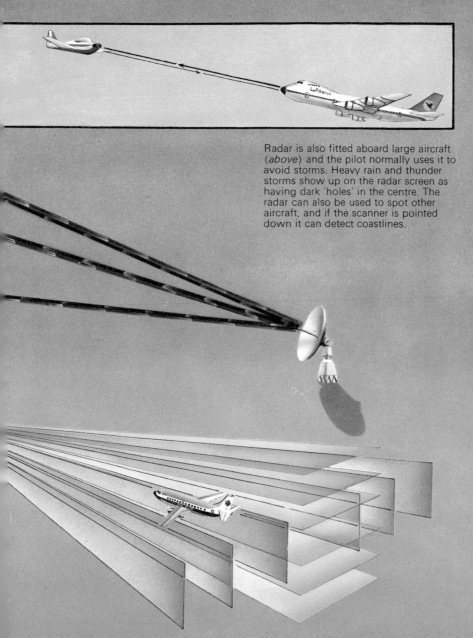

Radar is also fitted aboard large aircraft (*above*) and the pilot normally uses it to avoid storms. Heavy rain and thunder storms show up on the radar screen as having dark 'holes' in the centre. The radar can also be used to spot other aircraft, and if the scanner is pointed down it can detect coastlines.

During the flight the captain or co-pilot keeps the passengers informed of any point of interest over which they are flying, or simply gives general information about the aircraft height, speed and estimated arrival. Although maps are often provided to enable passengers to plot the course of the flight it is by no means easy to tell where you are when flying at 30,000 feet or so. One river or bay or even range of mountains is apt to look like another and it is easy to convince oneself that the piece of land below looks exactly like a certain point on the map, only to learn later that in fact the airliner is in quite a different position! Even when climbing out of or approaching a familiar city it can be remarkably difficult to pick out landmarks. The secret is to find just one known point (such as a railway station or a park) and then having got your bearings it is not so difficult to find other landmarks. Do not be disappointed if you fail to recognise anything even though you know that your own home is somewhere there below; even from a few thousand feet familiar places can look very different!

Right Avoid fatigue by wearing slippers, eating sparingly and resting on arrival.
Below A familiar road can look very different even from a thousand feet.

A word to a passenger can allay any anxieties she may have.

Though we have established that the crew up front have enough to keep them occupied, passengers are apt to get bored – especially on a flight which may last up to 24 hours – the flight time to Australia. Of course, on such a journey there will be at least one change of flight crews. At perhaps Bombay and Bangkok, the crews will be changed to ensure that fatigue does not diminish the alertness of those in charge of several hundred passengers.

Only passengers who fly very regularly are likely to learn ways of overcoming the tedium of long air journeys. Those with less experience are apt to add to their fatigue by doing the wrong thing. The excitement of undertaking a flight can itself be fatiguing. After all, a journey by air is an adventure and it may be difficult to relax, but you must try. Loose clothing will help, for as well as excitement, your body has to cope with the problems of altitude. A cabin pressure equivalent to 8,000 feet is quite adequate for a healthy person but some swelling is natural, so take off your shoes and wear slippers if you are embarking on a long journey. Tempting though the meals may be, do not overeat. Airlines provide meals partly to alleviate the boredom of long flights and special care is taken to make the appearance of the meal-trays attractive. It is not only your feet which will swell, your stomach too will expand a little, so avoid giving it too much to do!

The atmosphere in the cabin is apt to be rather dry and this can be combated by drinking more than normal. The temptation of too much duty-free alcohol, however, should be avoided as this serves only to increase dehydration.

Air sickness is a bogey which few passengers need fear. For the most part airliners fly in turbulence-free air at high altitudes, but even occasional bumpiness should not cause sickness. However, if you are prone to travel sickness, your doctor will advise on suitable preventatives.

In the days when a long journey by flying boat took several days, with nights spent in an hotel, the problems of the 'body clock' were unknown. With the advent of jet travel the importance of 'circadian rhythms' has been investigated by many experts. Even when shut away in a hut without daylight for a month, people will continue to live a pattern based on roughly a 24-hour cycle. Medical experiments

A wide-bodied airliner can be turned into a small cinema to entertain the passengers during a long flight.

A 'concert' or a magazine helps to while away otherwise tedious hours. Many passengers come prepared with a favourite book.

have proved this. When flying through many different time zones, the body understandably gets rather upset. Jetlag, as it has come to be called, affects different people in different ways – young folk seem to be less disturbed than others. Regardless of whether you feel fatigue after a long journey across time zones (that is to East or West) a rest in bed on arrival often helps acclimatization.

Airlines have thought of several ways to relieve the tedium of long distance travel. As well as providing frequent meals and snacks, they offer films, music and other entertainments. Using earphones (which usually have to be hired) a number of channels can be 'dialled' on a control panel in the armrest of the seat. Some airlines recommend exercises to keep the body in trim and language tuition is another diversion that is becoming increasingly popular with airline passengers.

The needs of very young passengers are often catered for in the shape of cuddly toys, games and books. Some airlines have formed clubs for older children, among them British Airways, British Caledonian, Lufthansa and Singapore Airlines. Oldest of them is the Junior Jet Club formed by BOAC in 1957 and now continued by British Airways. Members receive a badge and a log book in which to record their flights. Membership is limited to those who fly on long distance routes, and indeed the other airline clubs are principally for globe-trotters, too. The magazine 'Fleetwings' is circulated regularly to Junior Jet Club members and British Caledonian's Lion Club also produces a newspaper for its young members. The Lufthansa Junior Service provides a badge, log book and membership card for young passengers who fly regularly. These and other airlines will allow junior passengers to visit the flight deck if circumstances permit. On short journeys it is rarely possible to spend any time on the flight deck because the pilots are usually too busy. (Many short haul airliners have only two crew members, dispensing with the third pilot or the flight engineer.) If you do get an opportunity to see the crew at work, try to identify some of the flight instruments, such as the artificial horizon, the airspeed indicator and the altimeter.

As the flight progresses it is possible to keep in touch with the airline's operations base even if it is thousands of kilometres away. If the base wants to contact the aircrew for any reason it uses the Selcal communication system. This does not oblige the crew to 'listen out' on the company frequency all the time as a light or bell will indicate when the base is calling. On the flight deck the crew may be admiring the sun setting as a ball of red fire over the Ganges while the duty officer in the operations room back in Europe is pondering the chill weather of deep winter. Even if the airliner is on the ground it is possible to call the base thousands of kilometres away so that a technical problem may be discussed.

In radio communications, most airlines use their flight numbers as a call-sign; hence 'Swissair 167' or 'Alitalia 014'. Some airlines, however, maintain links with their earliest days by using special call-signs. 'Speedbird' for example, has been used by BOAC and now British Airways for many years. Pan American uses the call-sign 'Clipper,' perpetuating the name given to its flying boats during the 1930s.

Bizjets and private aircraft usually use their registration letters as a call-sign; 'Golf Bravo Bravo Lima Mike' would be used in full when calling the control tower but as soon as contact has been established the call-sign is usually reduced to 'Lima Mike'.

Words and phrases used on the radio are chosen so that there can be no misunderstanding in their use. 'Yes' and 'No' are never used. Instead 'affirmative' and 'negative' make the message absolutely clear. 'Roger' is a favourite of fiction writers when the subject of aircraft R/T (radio telephony) is introduced. It means, 'I have received all of your last transmission.' It is, in fact, rarely used.

The efforts to make flying safer are not restricted to the many check-lists and the duplicated or triplicated systems on board the aircraft. A considerable amount of emergency equipment is carried which will probably never be used. All high-flying jet airliners carry oxygen masks which, in the event of a failure in the pressurization, will automatically fall from the overhead racks to the passengers below. Oxygen starvation (hypoxia) can quickly bring about unconsciousness and its early symptoms are hard to diagnose. An initial lightheadedness much akin to drunkenness is followed quickly by a feeling of helplessness. The brain gives instructions but somehow one's limbs fail to respond. It is important therefore to use the oxygen masks quickly should they pop out from their containers. At the beginning of most flights safety instructions are demonstrated by the cabin crew. They point to the emergency exits, show how the oxygen masks should be used and demonstrate how to put on a life jacket. Flying is a very safe form of transport but accidents do happen and sometimes lives are needlessly lost because passengers do not know how to help themselves. The experienced passenger who 'knows it all' may well be the one who does not know what to do if an accident occurs for he has seen the emergency demonstration so many times that he does not really take any notice. You need not spoil the enjoyment of your journey by being anxious about the safety of the flight, but a sensible attention to the safety instructions would be wise. All sorts of strange equipment are carried on certain flights; on polar services, for example, in addition to the usual life rafts the aircraft carries polar survival suits, guns to deal with polar bears and special cold weather equipment.

It is important to remember to act quickly in the event of an emergency, for wasted seconds can mean the difference between life and death. If it becomes necessary to evacuate the aircraft, leave at once without any concern for your personal belongings. When the aircraft cabin is high off the ground inflatable chutes help to speed the exit from an airliner which has crash-landed. There have been some remarkable escapes from airliners which have become complete wrecks; speed has often been the key to survival.

Long before reaching its destination an airliner begins its descent –

under the guidance of air traffic controllers, of course. Some 160 kilometres or so from the airport, controllers will begin to plan the blending of several different aircraft into an orderly line for the approach to the runway. Different airliners operate at different heights; most jumbo-sized aircraft cruise at between 30,000 and 40,000 feet, smaller jets (which often perform relatively short journeys) fly between 20,000 and 30,000 feet, whilst yet smaller unpressurized aircraft fly at lower altitudes. Above them all at heights of up to 60,000 feet soar the Concorde and some executive jet aircraft.

It is rarely necessary to wear a life jacket in an aircraft but for a flight in a light 'plane or helicopter over water, it is a sensible precaution.

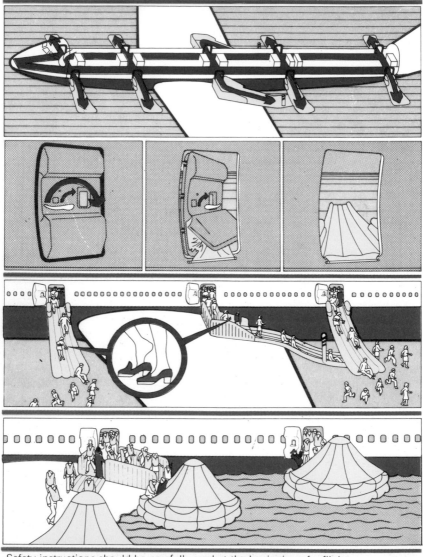

Safety instructions should be carefully read at the beginning of a flight.

F403 TRANSART INPLASTOR LTD PRINTED IN ENGLAND

As they all come together, the controllers begin to fit them into various patterns in the Terminal Control area. This is a large area in which all aircraft, except those below 3,000 feet or so, are under the control of the terminal radar. Navigation beacons dotted about the city are used as holding points from which the airliners descend until they can join the line of airliners leading to the airport. The controllers have a difficult choice, for in addition to weaving aircraft from different altitudes into the landing pattern they must consider the demands of departing aircraft and,

of course, they must channel airliners of different speeds into the flow. There are still piston-engined DC-3s occasionally to be seen approaching airports in the same queue as a Learjet and Boeing 707.

The area controller will hand over the inbound airliner to the approach controller who may well have to 'stack' the aircraft in a holding pattern over a VOR. *Gatwick Approach Danair 398 is descending to flight level 90, estimate Midhurst at 15.* Approaching from the south, the Danair HS 748 will descend to 9,000 feet and expects to be at the Midhurst VOR

Runway and taxi-way lighting has to be carefully monitored (*below left*) and air traffic controllers ensure that airliners are kept apart as they take-off and land

at 15 minutes past the hour. Slotted into the holding pattern, the 748 will take up a race-track pattern around the Midhurst beacon until the pilot is instructed to leave to join the queue of airliners waiting to land at Gatwick. When the bottleneck has cleared, the pilot will hear 'Danair 398 next time over Midhurst leave on a heading of 090 and descend to five thousand feet.' The 748 heads east passing Gatwick before turning back towards the west for a landing on runway 26 into the prevailing wind. The green countryside is covered with a mantle of patchy clouds and the passengers are given a tantalising glimpse of the towns down below: 'That must be Horsham – or is it Tunbridge Wells?' Even those familiar with the area will find it hard to identify a landmark before it slips beneath the wing or is covered by cloud again.

On the flight deck the check lists are out again and the approach speeds are monitored as the runway comes into view. The flaps are extended and the 748 descends gently to touch down on the runway, flashing past a giant Wardair Boeing 747 which is waiting to line up on the runway for a flight to Toronto.

Airways

To ensure the safe movement of airliners from city to city, each is kept at a certain distance, and height, from the others. Each step of the climb after take-off must be cleared by air traffic control and the airliner must follow an airway.

Far left The airways link airports with beacons along the route to the next city. Just like on a motorway, the traffic must obey the rules to ensure safety.

Above The progress of an airliner from one flight level to the next (measured in thousands of feet) must be cleared by an air traffic controller.

The controller in the tower carefully mixes the departing and arriving traffic, for much fuel can be wasted by aircraft held in the 'stack' at Midhurst or waiting for a turn to take off. A stray light aircraft en route to Biggin Hill can cause considerable disarray and wasted fuel. The London area is busy with arriving and departing airliners; Heathrow, Gatwick, Luton and Stanstead deal with the bulk of the traffic. Many smaller aircraft fly into and out of smaller airfields such as Elstree and Biggin Hill at heights of about 2,000 feet. These little Pipers and Cessnas must remain clear of the busy airports.

Although the sky may be clear and the visibility excellent, the airliners will always fly IFR – by Instrument Flight Rules. There is too much traffic to allow anyone to rely on seeing and being seen. After leaving the last beacon the approach controller will hand the landing aircraft over to the tower where another controller will guide the airliner on to the ILS beam. At the end of the runway a localizer beam sends signals which activate a cockpit instrument and guides the pilot to the centre-line of the runway. A glide path transmitter near the runway guides the airliner down, usually at an angle of 3 degrees. Be it in sunshine, in rain or at night, the pilot must put his passenger load safely on to a 75 metre wide strip of concrete. We have seen that even with all the high lift devices ex-

tended, control of an airliner at low speeds calls for precise and accurate flying. The Instrument Landing System is an invaluable aid to pilots who may have been airborne for over eight hours and are looking forward to a hot bath and a good night's rest. In the cabin, the passengers see the 'No Smoking' and 'Fasten Seat Belts' signs light up but those peering through the windows may see little through the thick cloud. 'Air India 119 heading 350 descend to 5,000 feet.' A Jumbo from Delhi is about to land at Frankfurt and the approach controller is guiding the pilot to a point where he can intercept the ILS radio beams. VHF transmitters located near the runway send signals to an aerial fixed to the nosewheel undercarriage door of the approaching Boeing 747. Coming from various directions, aircraft are fed into the locator beacon – a medium-wave radio beacon. With the radio compass needle aligned to the locator, the crew will know when they are passing over the beacon, for the needle will swing into the reverse direction. An outer marker signal beamed upwards from the beacon will also tell the pilots that they are on course by causing a bleeping noise and a flashing light on the flight deck and, in this case, the crew know they should be just over 1,400 feet above ground. The flaps are

Right As the runway comes into view all passengers and crew must fasten their seat belts and put out their cigarettes.

144

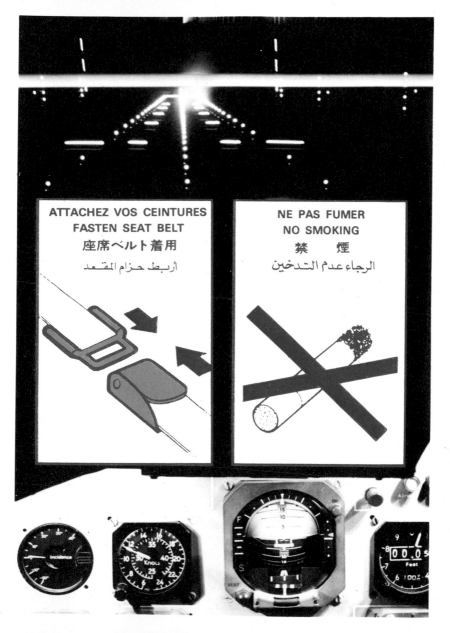

extended a little and the throttles opened to balance the increased drag. The instrument on the flight deck shows that the horizontal and vertical needles are crossed – the beams have been 'captured' and the great airliner is nearing the end of its journey, descending at a steady angle. A middle marker indicates that there is about a kilometre to go and the flight engineer calls out the height: 'Three hundred feet, two hundred feet.'

'Runway in sight,' announces the co-pilot, and the captain responds, 'Approach continued.' As the runway threshold is passed the rate of descent is checked, the nose being raised so that the bogies cushion the final few feet of the landing. As the runway lights flash by, reverse thrust is applied and, with a roar and a momentary shudder, some 300 tonnes of aeroplane are halted and the pilot steers the Boeing 747 clear of the runway. The passengers

A gentle touch and careful concentration are called for as a pilot brings Concorde to land.

This is the moment when a pilot has to exercise the greatest skill.

stir into life, the impatient ones foolishly ignoring the pleas of the cabin crew to remain seated until the aircraft has stopped. There is little to be gained by gathering coats and bags together in an endeavour to beat 300 other passengers off the aircraft! The groans and whines of the hydraulic system are heard again as the flaps are retracted and as the jumbo is gently taxied to its allotted stand, guided by lights or a 'follow me' vehicle, the pilot aligns his aircraft to a sign by the pier. Sometimes his positioning is aided by a marshaller who skilfully directs the pilot by using sticks or bats. His signals, like the radio instructions of the air traffic controller, are understood by all pilots.

Some specially equipped aircraft are able to land automatically using the ILS. If the ground installation is up to a certain standard, practically 'blind' landings can be made, a visibility of only 150 metres being required. (Much less and the pilot could not see to taxi to the airport terminal.) These Category III landings, as they are called, enable airliners to overcome the hazards presented by fog. Some airlines use automatic landing procedures even when the visibility is good, for it gives the crews an opportunity to practise in safe conditions so that when the weather is poor a 'blind' landing is mere routine.

Passengers can sometimes tell when an automatic landing is being made, for the autopilot is linked to the throttles which are constantly adjusted as the airport hoves into view. This rise and fall in the noise of the engines indicates that the autopilot is adjusting the speed for a perfect touch-down. The auto-throttle is usually engaged during a standard approach and landing as well. At just the right moment the autopilot cuts the power and the airliner sinks gently to the ground. B.E.A., now British Airways, has been a pioneer in the use of automatic landing systems and has amassed years of experience in making safe landings when other airlines have been obliged to cancel their services. No doubt many travel-weary businessmen have been grateful for this system on winter days.

this bay   move ahead   turn to port   turn to starboard

Docking an airliner

Top Aircraft marshallers help pilots to
steer their airliner to the parking position
on the apron.

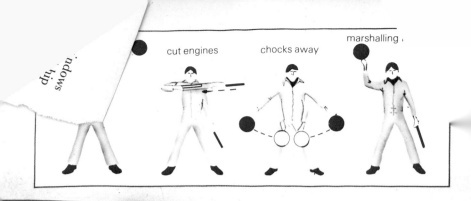

cut engines   chocks away   marshalling

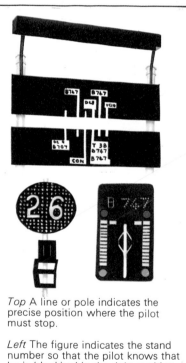

Top A line or pole indicates the precise position where the pilot must stop.

Left The figure indicates the stand number so that the pilot knows that he is 'docking' in the right position.

Right The lights indicate the correct 'docking' position; the central bar shows deviations left and right.

ou do not want to spend your journey tackling a book that I've always felt you should read – but never quite got round to – you would obviously be advised to seek a window seat in order to get the most enjoyment from the journey. A seat nearest the first class cabin is likely to be both the quietest part of the aircraft and to offer the best view. On jet aircraft the first class cabin is in the front, far away from the engine; with propeller-driven aircraft it is in the rear. The whirling propellers are usually rather noisy and so the first class passengers are accommodated in the rear. In either position the view of the ground is usually unimpeded by the wing.

Regardless of which window position you manage to get, there is bound to be something of interest to be seen. Over the wing you can watch the flaps, spoilers and ailerons at work. In front or behind the wing you can try your hand at finding your position on a map.

Airliners, of course, vary very much in size and shape. A wide-body aircraft has plenty of space to walk in but has a limited number of window seats. Many of the passengers have to sit in the centre areas where there is little opportunity to see out. In smaller aircraft such as the BAC One-Eleven or Boeing 737, it is usually possible to see something of the outside world. Yet smaller aircraft can offer quite splendid views; the Viscount has comparatively large oval and the Herald and Frien aircraft have high wings so tha everyone can see the ground.

A flight in a bizjet like the HS.125 or the Learjet is really like taking a ride in an aerial Rolls-Royce. Plush carpeting and leather upholstery provide the best in comfort, and often a stereo cassette player is on board to provide a selection of musical entertainment. After the long flexing wing of the Boeing 707, that of the bizjet seems tiny. The wingtip appears to be but a few feet away.

Inside the IL-62 (*top*) and the TU-144.

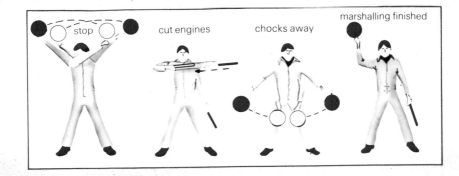

stop   cut engines   chocks away   marshalling finished

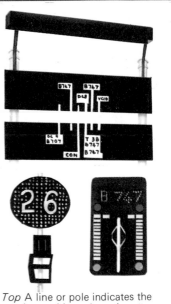

Top A line or pole indicates the precise position where the pilot must stop.

Left The figure indicates the stand number so that the pilot knows that he is 'docking' in the right position.

Right The lights indicate the correct 'docking' position; the central bar shows deviations left and right.

If you do not want to spend your air journey tackling a book that you've always felt you should read – but never quite got round to – you would obviously be advised to seek a window seat in order to get the most enjoyment from the journey. A seat nearest the first class cabin is likely to be both the quietest part of the aircraft and to offer the best view. On jet aircraft the first class cabin is in the front, far away from the engine; with propeller-driven aircraft it is in the rear. The whirling propellers are usually rather noisy and so the first class passengers are accommodated in the rear. In either position the view of the ground is usually unimpeded by the wing.

Regardless of which window position you manage to get, there is bound to be something of interest to be seen. Over the wing you can watch the flaps, spoilers and ailerons at work. In front or behind the wing you can try your hand at finding your position on a map.

Airliners, of course, vary very much in size and shape. A wide-body aircraft has plenty of space to walk in but has a limited number of window seats. Many of the passengers have to sit in the centre areas where there is little opportunity to see out. In smaller aircraft such as the BAC One-Eleven or Boeing 737, it is usually possible to see something of the outside world. Yet smaller aircraft can offer quite splendid views; the Viscount has comparatively large oval windows and the Herald and Friendship aircraft have high wings so that everyone can see the ground.

A flight in a bizjet like the HS.125 or the Learjet is really like taking a ride in an aerial Rolls-Royce. Plush carpeting and leather upholstery provide the best in comfort, and often a stereo cassette player is on board to provide a selection of musical entertainment. After the long flexing wing of the Boeing 707, that of the bizjet seems tiny. The wingtip appears to be but a few feet away.

Inside the IL-62 (*top*) and the TU-144.

Lunch-time in the economy class of a 747.

First class passengers enjoy a drink in the upper lounge of a Boeing 747.

The slender delta of the Concorde is also a marked contrast to a conventional airliner – the edge of the wing seems to be very close. The windows of the Concorde are very small because they must withstand the great pressures of high altitudes but after an hour or so (you will not be in it for very long) the little windows do not seem to be so very peculiar. When the Concorde is travelling at Mach 2, the windows heat up a little, (despite the outside temperature of −60°C,) giving some indication of the heat generated by the aircraft as it speeds along as fast as a bullet. Beyond the speed indicated by the Machmeter on the bulkheads in the passenger cabin, there is little sensation of speed, although as you watch the ground slipping by 60,000 feet below there is a greater sense of movement than there is in a subsonic jet.

Some may argue that a flight in a mini-airliner like the Britten-Norman Islander or a Bandeirante is the greatest fun. Every seat is a window seat and the aircraft flies quite close to the ground so that the view is excellent. It does tend to be rather bumpy because such aircraft cannot climb to the great heights of the jetliners. (As they are unpressurized you could not breathe if they did.) There is an informality and intimacy about such flights which is unique in airline travel. Small airliners usually fly on the less dense routes and so they are rarely to be seen at major airports such as Heathrow, Charles de Gaulle or Rome. The informality of the flight is repeated on the ground, therefore, and there are none of the lengthy boarding formalities associated with international travel on scheduled airlines.

| Mach 0·5 (around 530 km/hour) | Mach 0·9 (around 960 km/hour) | Mach 2 (around 2,000 km/hour) |

shockwave

As the aircraft approaches the speed of sound a shockwave forms.

Though Concorde (*above*) is less spacious than a DC-10 (*below*) passengers spend much less time on board Concorde.

In Scotland a service flown by the 14-seat Trislander involves a landing on the beach at Isle of Barra. Occasionally the fire engine has to be used to chase cattle away from the approach to the beach so that the little aircraft can land safely – puddles of sea-water splashing its side as it touches down.

But be it in a spacious TriStar or or a little Navajo, flying is an adventure which is enjoyed by a growing number of young air travellers throughout the world.

Civil aircraft of the world

There are, of course, many hundreds of different types of aircraft currently operated by airlines and other users. To include them all in this chapter would be impossible but most of those to be seen at or near major airports have been included in this section.

There is a curious mixture of metric and imperial measure in the aviation world. As the major producer of aeroplanes the United States has an understandable influence on current practice. For example, many aircraft produced in America have airspeed indicators calibrated in miles-per-hour, others use knots (nautical miles) – a more widely-accepted unit of measurement. Height on the altimeter is shown in feet although visibility along a runway is usually quoted in metres. On international flights the captain gives his 'progress report' to the passengers usually quoting both miles-per-hour as well as kilo-metres-per-hour and we have chosen to do the same.

We have given the maximum range with an average load (with an allowance for legally required diversions), the maximum take-off weight and the maximum cruising speed. These, of course, will not all be achieved together.

Every country which operates civil
aircraft has a means of identification
-- either letters or numbers.

AP	Pakistan	JY	Jordan
C	Canada	LN	Norway
CCCP	U.S.S.R.	LV	Argentina
CN	Morocco	LX	Luxembourg
CS	Portugal	LZ	Bulgaria
D	West Germany	N	U.S.A.
EC	Spain	OD	Lebanon
EI	Ireland	OE	Austria
EP	Iran	OH	Finland
ET	Ethiopia	OK	Czechoslovakia
F	France	OO	Belgium
G	United Kingdom	OY	Denmark
HA	Hungary	PH	Netherlands
HB	Switzerland	PK	Indonesia
HK	Columbia	PP	Brazil
HS	Thailand	PT	Brazil
HZ	Saudi Arabia	RP	Philippines
I	Italy	SE	Sweden
JA	Japan	SP	Poland

ST	Sudan	**4X**	Israel
SU	Egypt	**5A**	Libya
SX	Greece	**5B**	Cyprus
S2	Bangladesh	**5H**	Tanzania
TC	Turkey	**5N**	Nigeria
TF	Iceland	**5X**	Uganda
TS	Tunisia	**5Y**	Kenya
TU	Ivory Coast	**6O**	Somalia
VH	Australia	**6Y**	Jamaica
VT	India	**7Q**	Malawi
XA	Mexico	**7T**	Algeria
YA	Afghanistan	**9G**	Ghana
YI	Iraq	**9H**	Malta
YK	Syria	**9J**	Zambia
YR	Romania	**9K**	Kuwait
YU	Yugoslavia	**9M**	Malaysia
YV	Venezuela	**9Q**	Zaire
ZK	New Zealand	**9V**	Singapore
ZS	South Africa	**9Y**	Trinidad

Aero Spacelines AS.201 Super Guppy
Length 43·84m Wing span 47·62m Height
14·78m Max. take-off weight 77,110kg.
Max. cruising speed 463km/h (288mph)
Range 813km. Accommodation bulky cargo.
Power Plant 4 × Allison 501-D22C turboprops of 4912shp each. An astonishing
conversion of the Boeing Stratocruiser, the
Guppy aircraft are designed to carry bulky loads
and were originally used to carry rockets for
the U.S. space programme. Two are operated by
UTA to fly parts of the Airbus to the assembly
line in Toulouse.

Aerospatiale (Sud)SE210 Caravelle
Length 32m Wing span 34·3m Height 8·7m
Max. take-off weight 50,000kg Max. cruising
speed 845km/h (525mph) Range 2,300km
Accommodation up to 99 passengers. Power
plant 2 × Rolls Royce Avon turbo-jets of
12,600lb thrust. Entering service in 1959 the
Caravelle was the world's first rear-engine jet
airliner. Of the 280 built in several versions 133
remain in service – with 24 different airlines.

Aerospatiale SN601 Corvette Length
13·83m Wing span 12·87m Height 4·23m
Max. take-off weight 6600kg Max. cruising
speed 796km/h (495mph) Range 1645km
Accommodation up to 12 passengers Power
plant 2 × Pratt & Whitney JT15-D4 turbofans
of 2,310lb thrust. Operated as a 'third level'
airliner and as an executive jet only 40 of this
type were built.

Aerospatiale AS.350 Ecureuil Length
13·00m Rotor diameter 10·69m Height 3·08m.
Max. take-off weight 1,900kg Max. cruising
speed 230km/h (143mph) Range 845km
Accommodation up to 5 passengers Power
plant one Turbomeca Arriel (641shp) or one
Avco Lycoming LTS 101 turboshaft of 592shp.
Likely to be seen in increasing numbers in the
1980s, the 'Squirrel' has been produced as a
successor to the Alouette.

Aerospatiale/BAC Concorde Length
62·10m Wing span 25.56m Height 11·4m.
Max. take-off weight 185,070kg Max.
cruising speed 2150km/h (1330mph) Range
6,230km Accommodation 100 passengers
Power plant 4 × Rolls-Royce/SNECMA
Olympus 593 turbojets of 38,050lb thrust. The
world's only super-sonic jet transport in
regular scheduled service. Arguably the most
graceful airliner flying today, only 16
production Concordes have been built.

Agusta A.109A Hirundo Length 10·71m
Rotor diameter 11m Height 3·30m Max. take-
off weight 2,450kg Max. cruising speed
266km/h (165mph) Range 565km
Accommodation 7 passengers Power plant
2 × Allison 250-C20B turboshaft engines
rated at 420shp The first of the new generation
of sleek helicopters the Hirundo has a
retractable undercarriage.

Airbus A.300 (B2) Length 53·62m Wing span 44·84m Height 16·53m Max. take-off weight 142,000kg Max. cruising speed 911km/h (567mph) Range 3,334km Accommodation approx. 270 passengers plus under-floor cargo Power plant 2 × General Electric CF6-50C turbofans of 51,000lb thrust. Built by a consortium of European manufacturers, the Airbus is the first medium range 'wide body' airliner. Several versions of the A.300 are in service in many parts of the world.

Beechcraft B.99 Airliner Length 13·58m Wing span 14m Height 4·38m Max. take-off weight 4,944kg Max. cruising speed 451km/h (280mph) Range 600km Accommodation up to 17 seats Power plant 2 × Pratt & Whitney (Canada) PT6A-28 turbo-props of 680shp Produced as a 'third level' airliner, the Beech 99 is operated mainly in the United States although some are in use in Europe.

Airbus A.310 Length 46·15m Wing span 43·37m Height 15·78m Max. take-off weight 121,500kg Max. cruising speed 935km/h (583mph) Range 3,950km Accommodation 200 passengers Power plant 2 × General Electric CF6-45B2 turbofans of 51,000lb thrust A development of the larger A.300 Airbus, the A.310 has been ordered by Air France, Lufthansa and Swissair for operation in the 1980s.

Beechcraft Super King Air Length 13·36m Wing span 16·61m Height 4·52m Max. take-off weight 5,670kg Max. cruising speed 515km/h (320mph) Range 3,495km Accommodation up to 13 passengers Power plant 2 × Pratt & Whitney (Canada) PT6A-41 turbo-props of 850shp The latest of the King Air series first produced in 1964, the Super King Air is a popular executive transport aircraft.

Antonov An-24 Length 23·53m Wing span 29·20m Height 8·32m Max. take-off weight 21,000kg Max. cruising speed 450km/h (280mph) Range 2,400km Accommodation 44 passengers Power plant 2 × Ivchenko AI-24A turboprops of 2,550ehp Widely used by the Soviet airline Aeroflot as well as by other East European airlines, the An-24 has been produced in several versions, the total number exceeding 1,000.

Beechcraft 18 Length 10·70m Wing span 15·14m Max. take-off weight 4,490kg Cruising speed 354km/h (220mph) Range 2,460km Accommodation 9 passengers Power plant 2 Pratt & Whitney R-985 piston engines of 450 horsepower Pre-war light transport produced until 1969. Many tricycle under-carriage conversions are available.

Beechcraft Baron 58P Length 9·09m Wing span 11·53m Height 2·79m Max. take-off weight 2,785kg Max. cruising speed 427km/h (265mph) Range 2,309km Accommodation 5 passengers Power plant 2 × Continental TSIO-520L piston engines of 310hp This is the pressurised version of an aircraft used by many executive owner/pilots. Over 1,000 of the basic design have been produced.

Bell Model 206B Jet Ranger Length 9·5m Rotor diameter 10·16m Height 2·91m Max. take-off weight 1,451kg Max. cruising speed 219km/h (136mph) Range 624km Accommodation 4 passengers Power plant one Allison 250-C20B turboshaft rated at 420shp With over 5,000 produced this is one of the most widely used executive and general transport helicopters.

Bell Model 212 Length 12·92m Rotor diameter 14·69m Height 4·39m Max. take-off weight 5,080kg Max. cruising speed 203km/h (126mph) Range 439km Accommodation up to 14 passengers Power plant one Pratt & Whitney (Canada) PT6T-3 Twin Pac turbo-shaft rated at 1,250shp A development of the 'Huey' family which includes the Models 204, 205 and 214, the 212 is a general-purpose helicopter popular with off-shore oil rig support operators.

Bell Model 222 Length 10·98m Rotor diameter 12·12m Height 3·39m Max. take-off weight 3,470kg Max. cruising speed 265km/h (150mph) Range 644km Accommodation 9 passengers Power plant 2 × Avco Lycoming LTS 101-650C turbo-shaft engines rated at 600shp. Another of the new generation of sleek helicopters, this promises to enjoy world-wide success.

Boeing 707-720C Length 46·6m Wing span 44·42m Height 12·94m Max. take-off weight 151,315kg Max. cruising speed 965km/h (600mph) Range 6,920km Accommodation 189 passengers Power plant 4 × Pratt & Whitney JT3D-74 of 19,000lb thrust The first of the Boeing jet airliners, the 707 has remained in production for over 25 years. Several variants have been produced and further developments are in hand, one of which is a conversion to CFM-56 engines. Well over 900 707 airliners have been built, including the 720 version.

Boeing 727 Length 46·69m Wing span 32·92m Height 10·36m Max. take-off weight 95,027kg Max. cruising speed 964km/h (599mph) Range 3,966km Accommodation approximately 157 passengers Power plant 3 × Pratt & Whitney JT8D-17 of 16,000lb thrust With sales exceeding 1,600 and still climbing, this tri-jet is the most successful of all the jetliners.

Boeing 737 Length 30·48m Wing span 28·35m Height 11.28m Max. take-off weight 52,390kg. Max. cruising speed 927km/h (576mph) Range 3,521km Accommodation 115 passengers Power plant 2 × Pratt & Whitney JT8D-9A of 16,000lb thrust. A late entrant to the short-haul market, this baby of the Boeing family is still selling in large numbers.

Boeing 747-200B Length 70·51m Wing span 59·64m Height 19·33m Max. take-off weight 362,870kg Max. cruising speed 978km/h (608mph) Range 9,544km Accommodation Maximum of 500 passengers Power plant 4 × Pratt & Whitney JT9D-7F of 50,000lb thrust. Rolls-Royce or General Electric engines are also fitted. The first of the wide-body airliners, the Jumbo remains unchallenged as the largest airliner in the world. A smaller version – the 747SP – can can carry 360 passengers for 10,586km.

Boeing 757 Length 52·65m Wing span 37·94m Height 11·20m Max. take-off weight 99,790kg. Max. cruising speed 850km/h (530mph) Range 4,320km Accommodation up to 195 passengers Power plant 2 × Rolls-Royce RB211-535 turbo-fans of 36,600lb thrust General Electric CF6-32 or Pratt & Whitney JT10-D may be fitted. Developed from the Boeing 727, this airliner has a new wing, an extended fuselage and only two engines.

Boeing 767 Length 48·3m Wing span 47·24m Height 15·39m Max. take-off weight 126,937kg Max. cruising speed 850km/h (530mph) Range 4,075km Accommodation 208 passengers Power plant 2 × Pratt & Whitney JT9D-7R turbo-fans of 44,300lb thrust General Electric or Rolls-Royce engines may be fitted. This is the first completely new design produced by Boeing since the 747. United Airlines launched the type with an order for 30.

Boeing 777 Length 55·36 Wing span 47·24m Max. take-off weight 172,000kg Cruising speed 850km/h (530mph) Range 8,200km Accommodation 205 Power plant 2 General Electric CF6-80 engines. No 777s have as yet been built, but a number of major carriers have expressed interest in it.

Boeing Vertol Chinook Length 15·5m Diameter of each rotor 18·29m Height 5·7m Max. take-off weight 23,133kg Max. cruising speed 278km/h (173mph) Power plant 2 × Lycoming AL5512 turboshaft engines of 2,957shp Accommodation 44 passengers Range 1,010km British Airways have placed the first order for this civil version of a military helicopter and plan to use them for oil rig support services over the North Sea.

Bristol Britannia Length 37·87m Wing span 43·36m Height 11·43m Max. take-off weight 83,915kg Max. cruising speed 639km/h (397mph) Range 4,990km Accommodation 139 passengers or 15,650kg freight Power plant 4 × Bristol Proteus turboprops of 4,450shp Although not produced in large numbers the Britannia continues to give reliable service to several airlines.

British Aerospace (Avro later absorbed into Hawker Siddeley) 748 Length 20·42m Wing span 30·02m Height 7·57m Max. take-off weight 20,182kg Max. cruising speed 448km/h (278mph) Range 1,361km Accommodation up to 58 passengers Power plant 2 × Rolls-Royce Dart RDA7 turboprops of 2,280ehp First flown in 1960 this versatile transport continues in production.

British Aerospace (de Havilland later absorbed into Hawker Siddeley) 125 Length 15·46m Wing span 14·33m Height 5·36m Max. take-off weight 10,977kg Max. cruising speed 808km/h (502mph) Range 3,556km Accommodation 14 passengers Power plant 2 × Garrett TFE 731-3-1H turbofans of 3,700lb thrust For long one of the most successful of the executive jets, the BAe125 has been re-engined and stretched in recent years.

British Aerospace (Handley-Page) Jetstream 31 Length 14·35m Wing span 15·86m Height 5·30m Max. take-off weight 6,350kg Max. cruising speed 488km/h (303mph) Range 2,092km Accommodation up to 19 passengers Power plant 2 × Garrett TPE 331-10 turbo-props rated at 840shp The last design of the famous Handley-Page company, the Jetstream has recently been put back into production after a gap of several years.

British Aerospace (Hawker Siddeley) 146 Length 26·16m Wing span 26·36m Height 8·51m Max. take-off weight 33,500kg Max. cruising speed 790km/h (491mph) Range 1,177km Accommodation up to 88 passengers Power plant 4 × Avco Lycoming ALF502H of 6,700lb thrust First projected in the early 1970s this short-haul transport aircraft lay dormant until 1978 when it was revived by the new corporation. It is intended to replace earlier piston and turboprop-powered aircraft. A long fuselage version is planned.

BAC (Vickers) Super VC-10 Length 52·32m Wing span 44·55m Height 12·04m Max. take-off weight 151,950kg Max. cruising speed 935km/h (581mph) Range 7,600km Accommodation up to 174 passengers Power plant 4 × Rolls-Royce Conway Mk550 turbo-fans of 21,800lb thrust Designed for the 'Empire' routes of BOAC, the VC-10 and larger Super VC-10 proved to be very popular with passengers but these graceful airliners were overshadowed by their American rivals. Some retired VC-10s will continue to fly in the service of the RAF as tankers.

BAC One-Eleven 500 Length 32·61m
Wing span 28·5m Height 7·47m Max. take-off
weight 47,400kg Max. cruising speed 871km/h
(540mph) Range 2,744km Accommodation
119 passengers Power plant 2 × Rolls-Royce
Spey 512-DW turbo-fans of 12,550lb thrust
The 500 Series is the largest, although not the
latest, version of the One-Eleven. Although
over 200 (of all variants) have been sold, the
type has not enjoyed the success of its
American rival – the DC-9.

Canadair CL-44 Length 41·73m Wing
span 43·37m Height 11·80m Max. take-off
weight 95,250kg Max. cruising speed
621km/h (386mph) Range 5,245km
Accommodation 28,725kg of cargo or 200
passengers Power plant 4 × Rolls-Royce
Tyne turboprops of 5,730shp A development
of the Bristol Britannia, this cargo transport
features a swing tail to ease the loading of
bulky freight.

Britten-Norman Islander (now owned
by Pilatus) Length 10·86m Wing span 14·94m
Height 4·18m Max. take-off weight 2,993kg
Max. cruising speed 273km/h (160mph)
Range 1,400km Accommodation up to 9
passengers Power plant 2 × Lycoming 0-540
piston engines of 260hp A simple rugged
aircraft which is in service in many parts of the
world, sales of the Islander exceed 1,000.

Canadair CL-215 Length 19·82m Wing
span 28·60m Height 8·98m Max. take-off
weight 19,731kg Max. cruising speed 291km/h
(181mph) Range 2,260km Power plant 2 ×
Pratt & Whitney R-2800 piston engines of
2,100hp Role water bomber As a means of
controlling forest fires, the CL-215 has given
valuable service in such countries as Canada,
Spain, France and Greece.

Britten-Norman Trislander Length
15·01m Wing span 16·15m Height 4·11m
Max. take-off weight 4,536kg Max. cruising
speed 283km/h (176mph) Range 1,610km
Accommodation up to 17 passengers Power
plant 3 × Lycoming 0-540 piston engines of
260hp Big brother to the Islander, this three-
engined light transport is used by several small
operators.

Canadair Challenger Length 20·85m
Wing span 18·85m Height 6·01m Max. take-
off weight 14,755kg Max. cruising speed
935km/h (581mph) Range 5,185km
Accommodation up to 30 passengers Power
plant 2 × Avco Lycoming ALF 502 turbofans
of 7,500lb thrust A new-generation 'jumbo'
bizjet, this Canadian aircraft was the brain-
child of Bill Lear of Learjet fame.

Casa Aviocar Length 15·20m Wing span 19·0m Height 6·30m Max. take-off weight 6,500kg Max. cruising speed 359km/h (196mph) Range 480km. Accommodation 19 passengers or 2,000kg of freight Power plant 2 × Garrett TPE331 turboprops of 750shp. The first Spanish transport aircraft to sell on world markets, this rugged design can carry bulky loads.

Cessna 172 Skyhawk 2 Length 8·20m Wing span 10·92m Height 2·68m Max. take-off weight 1,043kg Max. cruising speed 232km/h (144mph) Range 900km Accommodation 3 passengers Power plant 1 Lycoming 0-320 piston engine of 160hp. One of the most commonly used private/training aircraft with over 25,000 examples built.

Cessna 337 Skymaster Length 9·07m Wing span 11·63m Height 2·79m Max. take-off weight 2,100kg. Max. cruising speed 314km/h (195mph) Range 1,241km. Accommodation 5 passengers Power plant 2 × Continental I0-360-G piston engines of 210hp. Unusual in having two engines in a 'fore and aft' position, the Skymaster is used as a private or taxi transport. Some 2,000 examples have been built to date.

Cessna 421 Golden Eagle Length 11·09m Wing span 12·53m Height 3·49m Max. take-off weight 3,379kg Max. cruising speed 445km/h (276mph) Range 2,755km Accommodation 7 passengers Power plant 2 × Continental GT-SI0-520 piston engines of 375hp. Cessna have built many different types of twin-engined executive and 'third level' transport aircraft. The Golden Eagle may be regarded as typical of the company's executive aircraft.

Cessna Titan Length 12·04m Wing span 14·12m Height 3·99m Max. take-off weight 3,705kg Max. cruising speed 404km/h (257mph) Range 3,402km Accommodation up to 9 passengers Power plant 2 × Continental GTSI0-520 piston engines of 375hp Another executive or 'commuter' transport the Titan is used by some airlines to pioneer new routes.

Cessna Citation I Length 13·27m Wing span 14·36m Height 4·37m Max. take-off weight 5,375kg Max. cruising speed 650km/h (404mph) Range 2,470km Accommodation 6 passengers Power plant 2 × Pratt & Whitney JT15D turbofans of 2,200lb thrust Although a relatively recent entrant on to the bizjet market, the Citation is selling well and has been developed into larger versions.

Convair 580 Length 24·84m Wing span
32·12m Height 8·59m Max. take-off weight
24,950kg Max. cruising speed 482km/h
(300mph) Range 2,980km Accommodation
44 passengers Power plant 2 × Allison 501
turboprops of 3,750shp. There have been
several turboprop conversions of the piston-
engined Convair 240/340/440 family but the
580 is the type which is in widest use.

Dassault Mercure Length 34·84m
Wing span 30·55m Height 11:36m Max. take-
off weight 56,500kg Max. cruising speed
932km/h (579mph) Range 750km
Accommodation 150 passengers Power plant
2 × Pratt & Whitney JT8-D15 turbofans of
15,500lb thrust Only ten of these airliners were
built for service with Air Inter in France.
Intended to compete with the Boeing 737 it
failed to attract orders at a time when the world
economy was depressed.

Convair 990A Length 42·43m Wing span
36·58m Height 12·04m Max. take-off weight
114,760kg Max. cruising speed 990km/h
(615mph) Range 6,115km Accommodation
149 passengers Power plant 4 × General
Electric CJ805-23B turbofans of 16,050lb
thrust Developed from the Convair 880 this
fast airliner was not built in substantial numbers
and failed to match the success of the Boeing
707 and Douglas DC-8. Some remain in
service with Spantax – a Spanish charter
airline.

Dassault-Breguet Mystère Falcon 20
Length 17·15m Wing span 16·30m Height
5·32m Max. take-off weight 13,000kg Max.
cruising speed 862km/h (536mph) Range
3,350km Accommodation up to 14 passengers
Power plant 2 × General Electric CF700
turbofans of 4,500lb thrust. One of the first
bizjets and also one of the most successful with
sales of well over 400. A smaller development –
the Falcon 10 – carries seven passengers.

Curtiss C-46 Length 23·27m Wing span
32·92m Height 6·60m Max. take-off weight
21,772kg Max. cruising speed 301km/h
(187mph) Range 2,117km Accommodation
up to 62 passengers or over 5,000kg freight
Power plant 2 × Pratt & Whitney R-2,800
piston engines of 2,000hp This type first flew
in 1940 but a number are still in use – mainly
in the United States.

Dassault-Breguet Mystère Falcon 50
Length 18·43m Wing span 18·86m Height
6·97m Max. take-off weight 17,000kg. Max.
cruising speed 870km/h (540mph) Range
6,295km Accommodation 10 passengers
Power plant 3 × Garrett TFE731 turbofans of
3,700lb thrust A new-generation executive jet
which is capable of flying trans-Atlantic
routes.

de Havilland Heron
Length 14·75m Wing span 21·7m Height 4·7m Max. take-weight 5,896kg Max. cruising speed 293km/h (183mph) Range 1,290km Accommodation up to 17 passengers Power plant 4 × de Havilland Gipsy Queen piston engines of 250hp. Examples of this 30-year-old design are still in use with executive or 'third level' operators A modification, the Saunders ST 27, is shown.

de Havilland Canada Dash Seven
Length 24·50m Wing span 28·35m Height 8·00m Max. take-off weight 19,504kg. Max. cruising speed 436km/h (281mph) Range 1,504km Accommodation up to 54 passengers Power plant 4 × Pratt & Whitney (Canada) PT6A-50 turboprops of 1,120shp The largest of the de Havilland STOL family, the Dash Seven has been designed to provide more accommodation on routes previously served by small STOL aircraft.

de Havilland Canada DHC 2 Beaver
Length 10·75m Wing span 14·64m Max. take-off weight 2,435kg Cruising speed 252km/h (157mph) Range 1,090km Accommodation 10 passengers Power plant 1 Pratt & Whitney R-985 radial engine of 450 horsepower. Rugged utility aircraft, sometimes equipped with skis for operation in Arctic conditions.

Douglas DC-3
Length 19·66m Wing span 28·96m Height 5·16m Max. take-off weight 11,430kg Max. cruising speed 312km/h (194mph) Range 563km Accommodation up to 28 passengers Power plant 2 × Pratt & Whitney R-1830 Twin Wasp piston engines of 1,200hp Father of the modern airliner and still going strong 40 years after entering service. Over 10,000 were built and some 1,000 remain in use.

de Havilland Canada DHC-6 Twin Otter
Length 15·77m Wing span 19·81m Height 5·66m Max. take-off weight 5,670kg Max. cruising speed 338km/h (210mph) Range 1,435km Accommodation up to 20 passengers Power plant 2 × Pratt & Whitney (Canada) PT6A-27 turboprops of 652ehp. A highly successful 'third level' and bush transport, the Twin Otter was developed from the single-engined Otter.

Douglas DC-6B
Length 32·2m Wing span 35·81m Height 8·92m Max. take-off weight 48,534kg Max. cruising speed 509km/h (316mph) Range 4,828km Accommodation 90 passengers Power plant 4 × Pratt & Whitney R-2800 piston engines of 2,500hp Developed from the DC-4 the DC-6 was a very successful airliner. Over 100 remain in service, mostly with charter airlines.

Dornier Skyservant Length 11·41m Wing span 15·55m Height 3·90m Max. take-off weight 3,842kg Max. cruising speed 273km/h (170mph) Range over 2,000km Accommodation up to 14 passengers Power plant 2 × Lycoming IGSO-540 piston engines of 380hp This STOL transport aircraft is used by bush operators in many parts of the world. A turbo-prop version is under development.

Embraer 11OP2 Bandeirante Length 15·1m Wing span 15·32m Height 4·73m Max. take-off weight 5,670kg Max. cruising speed 417km/h (259mph) Range 2,050km Accommodation 21 passengers Power plant 2 × Pratt & Whitney (Canada) PT6A-34 turbo-props of 750shp A successful 'third level' airliner which has established Brazil as an aircraft-exporting nation.

Embraer Xingu Length 11·01m Wing span 14·14m Height 4·94m Max. take-off weight 5,600kg Max. cruising speed 467km/h (290mph) Range 2,410km Accommodation 19 passengers Power plant 2 × Pratt & Whitney (Canada) PT6A-28 turboprops of 680shp An executive transport, the Xingu has a pressurized cabin.

Fairchild Swearingen Metro II Length 18·09m Wing span 14·10m Height 5·08m Max. take-off weight 5,670kg Max. cruising speed 473km/h (294mph) Range 346km Accommodation 19 passengers Power plant 2 × Garrett TPE 331 turboprops of 940shp Notable for its long slender fuselage, the Metro II is enjoying some success as a 'third level' transport.

Fokker Friendship F27 Length 23·56m Wing span 29·0m Height 8·41m Max. take-off weight 20,410kg Max. cruising speed 486km/h (302mph) Range 1,930km Accommodation 44 passengers Power plant 2 × Rolls-Royce Dart 532 turboprops of 2,140shp The first — and with over 600 sold — the most successful, of the twin turbo-prop short/medium range airliners. It has been produced in various versions and was manufactured under licence by Fairchild in the United States.

Fokker Fellowship F28 Length 29·61m Wing span 25·07m Height 8·47m Max. take-off weight 32,200kg Max. cruising speed 849km/h (528mph) Range 1,852km Accommodation 85 passengers Power plant 2 × Rolls-Royce Spey 555 turbofans of 9,850lb thrust Although over 100 have been sold this Dutch airliner has not enjoyed the same success as the Friendship. It is nevertheless popular with airlines using rough airstrips.

Gates Learjet 35 Length 14·83m Wing span 12·04m Height 3·73m Max. take-off weight 7711kg. Max. cruising speed 859km/h (534mph) Range 4,276km. Accommodation up to 8 passengers Power plant 2 × Garrett TFE 731-2 turbofans of 3,500lb thrust This is a variant of what is arguably the best-looking bizjet; the Learjet is also the best selling executive aircraft.

Grumman Goose Length 12·07m Wing span 15·40m Max. take-off weight 3,628kg Cruising speed 320km/h (200 mph) Range 1,600km Accommodation 10 passengers Power plant 2 Pratt & Whitney Wasp Junior engines of 450 horsepower. Amphibious transport capable of landing on water or land. The turbo-Goose is a turbo-prop conversion with improved performance.

Goodyear Europa Length 58·67m Width 15·24m Height 18·14m Max. take-off weight 5,824kg Max. cruising speed 80km/h (50mph) Max. endurance 23 hours Accommodation 6 passengers Power plant 2 × Continental IO-360 piston engines of 210hp Used mainly as an aerial platform from which to televise sports events, etc., the Europa airship tours Western Europe in the Spring and Summer months.

Grumman Gulfstream 1
Length 19·43m Wing span 23·92m Height 6·94m Max. take-off weight 15,920kg Max. cruising speed 560km/h (348mph) Range 4,058km. Accommodation up to 24 passengers Power plant 2 × Rolls-Royce Dart 529 turbo-props of 2,210shp A popular executive transport aircraft which is still in widespread use although production ended in 1969. A jet version powered by Rolls-Royce Speys is now produced by the Gulfstream American Corporation.

GAF Nomad Length 12·56m Wing span 16·46m Height 5·52m Max. take-off weight 3,855kg Max. cruising speed 311km/h (193mph) Range 1,352km Accommodation 14 passengers Power plant 2 × Allison 250-B17B turboprops of 400shp An Australian design which is enjoying some success in third world countries as a bush transport. The Nomad has an excellent STOL performance and has been developed into a larger 17-seat version.

Gulfstream American Hustler 500
Length 12·49m Wing span 10·49m Height 3·99m Max. take-off weight 4,313kg Max. cruising speed 740km/h (460mph) Range approx. 3,690km Accommodation 7 passengers Power plant 1 Garrett TPE 331-10-501 of 900 shp in the nose and one Pratt & Whitney Canada JT15D-1 turbo-fan of 2,200lb thrust in the tail Unusual in combining jet and turbo-prop power the Hustler is an executive transport aircraft.

Handley Page Herald Length 23·01m
Wing span 28·88m Height 7·34m Max. take-off
weight 19,505kg Max. cruising speed 441km/h
(274mph) Range 1,125km. Accommodation
56 passengers Power plant 2 × Rolls-Royce
Dart 527 turboprops of 2,105shp Few of these
airliners were built although a number remain
in service – mostly with some British
independent airlines.

**Hawker Siddeley (de Havilland)
Trident 3** Length 39·98m Wing span 29·87m
Height 8·61m Max. take-off weight 68,040kg
Max. cruising speed 967km/h (601mph)
Range 2,200km Accommodation 150
passengers Power plant 3 × Rolls-Royce
Spey 512 turbofans of 11,960lb thrust plus
an RB162 booster jet (5,250lbs) in the tail.
The last of the Trident series, this high capacity
version is in use (along with earlier marks)
with British Airways and C.A.A.C.

**Hawker Siddeley (de Havilland)
Comet 4** Length 35·97m Wing span 35m
Max. take-off weight 73,500kg Cruising speed
872km/h (542mph) Range 4,168km
Accommodation 101 passengers Power plant
4 Rolls-Royce Avon turbo-jets of 10,500lbs
thrust. Development of the Comet 1, which was
the world's first jet airliner, the Comet 4 was
produced in several versions for long haul, short
haul and military use.

Hughes 500D Length 9·30m Rotor
diameter 8·05m Height 2·53m Max. take-off
weight 1,360kg Max. cruising speed 258km/h
(160mph) Range 482km Accommodation 4
passengers Power plant 1 Allison 250-C20B
turboshaft of 420shp This 'flying tadpole' has
been built in large numbers for use as an
executive and general transport.

**Hawker Siddeley (de Havilland)
Dove** Length 12·30m Wing span 17·37m Max.
take-off weight 3,855kg Cruising speed
336km/h (210mph) Range 800km
Accommodation 10 passengers Power plant
2 de Havilland Gipsy Queen piston engines of
330 horsepower. Built as a light transport, these
aircraft are still in service as military
communications aircraft and as executive
models. Some have been converted to turbo-
prop power.

Ilyushin Il-18 Length 35·90m Wing span
37·40m Height 10·17m Max. take-off weight
64,000kg Max. cruising speed 675km/h
(419mph) Range 3,700km Accommodation
up to 122 passengers Power plant 4 ×
Ivchenko AI-20M turboprops of 4,250ehp
Several hundred of this Russian transport
aircraft are still in service, the first having
begun scheduled flying in 1959.

Ilyushin Il-62 Length 53·12m Wing span 43·20m Height 12·35m Max. take-off weight 162,000kg Max. cruising speed 900km/h (560mph) Range 6,700km. Accommodation up to 186 passengers Power plant 4 × Kuznetsov NK-8-4 turbofans of 23,150lb thrust Similar in appearance to the British VC-10, this Russian long range airliner is in service with several Soviet countries.

Let 410 Turbolet Length 13·61m Wing span 17·48m Height 5·65m Max. take-off weight 5,700kg. Max. cruising speed 370km/h (230mph) Range 1,300km Accommodation 19 passengers Power plant 2 × Pratt & Whitney (Canada) PT6A-27 turboprops of 715shp This Czechoslovakian feeder liner has also been produced with Walter M601 turboprops for Soviet bloc operators.

Ilyushin Il-86 Length 58·50m Wing span 48·33m Height 15·70m Max. take-off weight 188,000kg Max. cruising speed 950km/h (590mph) Range 3,800km Accommodation approx. 350 passengers Power plant 4 × Kuznetsov NK-86 turbofans of 28,635lb thrust The first Soviet wide body airliner, the Il-86 is unusual in featuring airstairs which enable passengers to board beneath the main cabin floor and deposit their baggage.

Lockheed Electra Length 31·81m Wing span 30·18m Height 10·0m Max. take-off weight 52,664kg Max. cruising speed 652km/h (405mph) Range 3,540km Accommodation 100 + passengers Power plant 4 × Allison 501 turboprops of 3,750shp This medium-range airliner first entered service over 20 years ago and those that remain in use are operated mostly by charter airlines.

IAI Westwind Length 15·93m Wing span 13·65m Height 4·81m Max. take-off weight 10,364kg Max. cruising speed 872km/h (542mph) Range 4,490km Accommodation up to 10 passengers Power plant 2 × Garrett TFE 731-3 turbofans of 3,700lb thrust This design began life in the United States but was sold to IAI in the early 1970s. New developments have been produced in recent years.

Lockheed JetStar Length 18·42m Wing span 16·60m Height 6·23m Max. take-off weight 20,185kg Max. cruising speed 880km/h (547mph) Range 4,818km Accommodation 10 passengers Power plant 4 × Garrett TFE 731-3 turbofans of 3,700lb thrust The first purpose-built long range executive jet, the JetStar continues in production.

Lockheed TriStar Length 54·35m Wing span 47·34m Height 16·87m Max. take-off weight 195,045kg Max. cruising speed 964km/h (599mph) Range 5,319km Accommodation 345 + passengers Power plant 3 × Rolls-Royce RB.211-22B turbofans of 42,000lb thrust This wide-bodied airliner has had a chequered career but it has continued to win orders including a crucial contract from Pan Am, for the latest -500, a shorter aircraft with bigger engines and greater range.

McDonnell Douglas DC-10 Length 55·5m Wing span 50·42m Height 17·7m Max. take-off weight 259,450kg Max. cruising speed 908km/h (564mph) Range 7,413km Accommodation up to 380 passengers Power plant 3 × General Electric CF6-50C turbofans of 52,500lb thrust A very successful wide-bodied airliner which is in service with airlines in many parts of the world.

McDonnell Douglas DC-8 Length 57·12m Wing span 45·23m Height 12·92m Max. take-off weight 158,760kg Max. cruising speed 965km/h (600mph) Range 7,240km Accommodation up to 259 passengers Power plant 4 × Pratt & Whitney JT3D-7 turbofans of 17,000lb thrust This 'stretched' version of the DC-8 is regarded as one of the most efficient airliners built although most are now operated by charter airlines. Many earlier models have been converted for all-cargo operations.

MBB Bo105 Length 8·55m Rotor diameter 9·82m Height 2·98m Max. take-off weight 2,300kg Max. cruising speed 245km/h (152mph) Range 656km Accommodation 4 passengers Power plant 2 × Allison 250-C20 turboshafts of 420shp. This German helicopter is in service in many parts of the world — mainly as an executive transport.

McDonnell-Douglas DC-9 Super 80 Length 45·08m Wing span 32·85m Height 8·93m Max. take-off weight 63,503kg Max. cruising speed 898km/h (558mph) Range 3,817km Accommodation up to 172 passengers Power plant 2 × Pratt & Whitney JT8D-209 turbofans of 18,500lb thrust Steadily refined since its introduction in 1967. The first version – the Series 10 – could carry 72 passengers. Sales of the DC-9 seem certain to exceed 1,000.

Mitsubishi MU-2 Length 10·13m Wing span 11·94m Height 3·94m Max. take-off weight 4,750kg. Max. cruising speed 587km/h (365mph) Range 2,705km Accommodation 7 passengers Power plant 2 × Garrett TPE 331 turboprops of 724ehp Over 500 of these Japanese executive aircraft have been sold. Several different models have been produced including a long-fuselage, 10-passenger variant.

NAMC YS-11 Length 26·30m Wing span 32.00m Height 8·98m Max. take-off weight 24,500kg Max. cruising speed 469km/h (291mph) Range 1,090km. Accommodation 60 passengers Power plant 2 × Rolls-Royce Dart 542 turboprops of 3,060ehp Built by a consortium of Japanese manufacturers, the YS-11 was not sold in large numbers. Over 100 remain in service, however.

Piper (Cherokee) Warrior PA28 Length 7·25m Wing span 10·67m Height 2·22m Max. take-off weight 1,054kg. Max. cruising speed 235km/h (146mph) Range 1,158km. Accommodation 4 seats Power plant 1 Lycoming 0-320 piston engine of 160hp Produced in large numbers and many versions, the Cherokee is often flown by businessmen and is occasionally to be seen at major airports.

Partenavia P.68B Length 9·35m Wing span 12·00m Height 3·40m Max. take-off weight 1,960kg. Max. cruising speed 302km/h (188mph) Range 1,681km Accommodation 6 passengers Power plant 2 × Lycoming IO-360 piston engines of 200hp An elegant light transport, this Italian design is being used as a taxi and executive aircraft.

Piper PA23 Aztec Length 9·52m Wing span 11·34m Height 3·15m Max. take-off weight 2,360kg. Max. cruising speed 338km/h (210mph) Range 2,445km Accommodation 5 passengers Power plant 2 × Lycoming IO-540 piston engines of 250hp Over 4,000 of these taxi/executive aircraft have been sold and the type is a familiar sight at many of the world's airports.

Piaggio P.166-DL3 Length 11·90m Wing span 14·69m Height 5·0m Max. take-off weight 4,300kg. Max. cruising speed 404km/h (250mph) Range 741km Accommodation 8 passengers Power plant 2 × Lycoming LTP-101 turboprops of 587shp This design is over 20 years old and is unusual in featuring pusher engines. The turboprop version is the most recent variant.

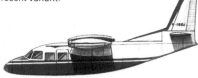

Piper PA35 Chieftan Length 9·94m Wing span 12·40m Height 3·96m Max. take-off weight 3,175kg. Max. cruising speed 410km/h (254mph) Range 1,640km Accommodation 6 passengers Power plant 2 × Lycoming TIO-540 piston engines of 350hp. The Chieftan is a lengthened version of the Navajo. A very popular taxi and third level transport aircraft; over 2,000 have been produced. It has been developed into the Cheyenne turboprop transport.

Piper PA34 Seneca Length 8·73m Wing span 11·85m Height 3·02m Max. take-off weight 2,073kg Max. cruising speed 352km/h (219mph) Range 1,129km Accommodation 5 passengers Power plant 2 × Continental TSI0-360 piston engines of 200hp. A widely-used light transport, the Seneca has been licence-produced in Brazil and Poland.

Rockwell Turbo Commander Length 13·52m Wing span 14·22m Height 4·56m Max. take-off weight 4,649kg Max. cruising speed 532km/h (330mph) Range 1,370km Accommodation 6 passengers Power plant 2 × Gàrett TPE 331 turboprops of 700ehp A development of the Aero Commander, a classic executive and light transport aircraft in service widely throughout the world.

Piper PA 601 B Aerostar (formerly Ted Smith) Length 10·61m Wing span 11·18m Height 3·70m Max. take-off weight 2,721kg Max. cruising speed 486km/h (302mph) Range 2,309km Accommodation 5 passengers Power plant 2 × Lycoming I0-540 piston engines of 290hp A fast and popular executive aircraft designed by the late Ted Smith.

Rockwell Sabreliner 75A Length 14·34m Wing span 13·62m Height 5·26m Max. take-off weight 10,580kg. Max. cruising speed 906km/h (563mph) Range 3,156km Accommodation up to 10 passengers Power plant 2 × General Electric CF-700 turbofans of 4,500lb thrust Most of the early Sabreliners were used by military operators. In recent years the type has become a popular bizjet.

Pitts S-2A Special Length 5·41m Wing span 6·10m Height 1·94m Max. take-off weight 680kg Max. cruising speed 245km/h (152mph) Range 552km Role aerobatic Power plant 1 Lycoming AE10-360 piston engine of 200hp Popular as a team aerobatic aeroplane, this aircraft is occasionally to be seen at air displays. The Rothmans Aerobatic Team is the most famous operator of the type.

Rockwell/Fuji Commander 700 Length 12·00m Wing span 12·94m Height 3·90m Max. take-off weight 2,993kg Max. cruising speed 405km/h (252mph) Range 1,926km Accommodation up to 6 passengers Power plant 2 × Lycoming TI0-540 piston engines of 325hp Designed by Fuji, this aircraft has been developed for production in both Japan and the United States.

Shorts 330 Length 17·69m Wing span 22·78m Height 4·78m Max. take-off weight 9,979kg Max. cruising speed 367km/h (228mph) Range 814km Accommodation 30 passengers Power plant 2 × Pratt & Whitney (Canada) PT6A-45 turboprops of 1,120shp Developed from the Skyvan freighter, the 330 is a new generation 'third level' airliner — reputed to be one of the quietest.

Sikorsky S-76 Length 13·44m Rotor diameter 13·41m Height 4·41m Max. take-off weight 4,399kg Max. cruising speed 269km/h (167mph) Range 742km Accommodation up to 12 passengers Power plant 2 × Allison 250-C30 turboshafts of 650shp A new generation transport helicopter this type promises to see wide service as an executive and oil rig support transport.

Sikorsky S-58 Length 14·40m Rotor diameter 17·07m Height 4·85m Max. take-off weight 5896kg Max. cruising speed 204km/h (127mph) Range 447km Accommodation up to 16 passengers Power plant 1 Pratt & Whitney (Canada) PT6T-6 Twin Pac of 1,875shp The S-58 has been produced in several versions since the early 1950s. The S-58T is in use over the North Sea on oil rig support services.

Tupolev Tu134 Length 34·35m Wing span 29·00m Height 9·02m Max. take-off weight 44,500kg Max. cruising speed 900km/h (559mph) Range 2,400km Accommodation up to 80 passengers Power plant 2 × Soloviev D-30 turbofans of 14,490lb thrust In use by many Eastern bloc air lines, this Russian design is in the DC-9/One-Eleven category.

Sikorsky S-61N Length 17·96m Rotor diameter 18·90m Height 5·63m Max. take-off weight 9,300kg Max. cruising speed 222km/h (138mph) Range 796km Accommodation up to 30 passengers Power plant 2 × General Electric CT58 turboshaft engines of 1,500shp This type has brought scheduled helicopter operations to several parts of the world.

Tupolev Tu 144 Length 65·70m Wing span 28·80m Max. take-off weight 180,000kg Cruising speed 2,500km/h (1,550mph) Range 6,500km Accommodation 140 passengers maximum Power plant 4 Kuznetzov NK 144 turbo-fan engines of 44,090lbs thrust with after-burning. The first supersonic passenger aircraft to fly, the Tu 144 has not yet entered regular passenger service and several are believed to have crashed during testing.

Tupolev Tu154 Length 47·90m Wing span 37·55m Height 11·40m Max. take-off weight 90,000kg Max. cruising speed 975km/h (605mph) Range 3,460km Accommodation up to 164 passengers Power plant 3 × Kuznetsov NK-8-2 turbofans of 20,950lb thrust Similar to the Trident and Boeing 727 of the West, this tri-jet is used by several Soviet airlines.

VFW Fokker VFW 614 Length 20·60m Wing span 21·50m Max. take-off weight 19,950kg Cruising speed 704km/h (438mph) Range 1,204km Accommodation 44 passengers Power plant 2 Rolls-Royce M45H turbo-fan engines of 7,280lbs thrust. An unsuccessful design for a quiet short-range airliner, which sold only a few examples.

Vickers Viscount Length 26·11m Wing span 28·50m Height 8·16m Max. take-off weight 32,886kg. Max. cruising speed 563km/h (350mph) Range 2,775km Accommodation 71 passengers Power plant 4 × Rolls-Royce Dart 525 turboprops of 2,100ehp A pioneer of turbo-prop air transport, the Viscount still remains in service.

Yakovlev Yak-40 Length 20·36m Wing span 25·0m Height 6·50m Max. take-off weight 16,000kg Max. cruising speed 550km/h (342mph) Range 1,450km Accommodation 33 passengers Power plant 3 × Ivchenko AI-25 turbofans of 3,300lb thrust Nearly 1,000 of these short-haul transports have been built. Designed to replace the Russian version of the DC-3 (the Lisunov Li-2), this tri-jet can be operated from grass strips.

Vickers Vanguard Length 37·45m Wing span 36·15m Height 10·64m Max. take-off weight 64,410kg Max. cruising speed 684km/h (425mph) Range 2,945km Accommodation 139 passengers Power plant 4 × Rolls-Royce Tyne 512 turboprops of 5,545ehp This big brother to the Viscount did not enjoy the same success. Only a few remain in service.

Yakovlev Yak-42 Length 36·38m Wing span 34·20m Height 9·83m Max. take-off weight 52,000kg. Max. cruising speed 870km/h (540mph) Range 1,000km Accommodation 120 passengers Power plant 3 × Lotarev D-36 turbofans of 14,200lb thrust Over 200 are to be supplied to Aeroflot and many more are certain to be manufactured in the coming years.

Military aircraft of the world

The aircraft described in this chapter are sometimes to be seen at international airports. Most are 'passive' aircraft such as transports, trainers and helicopters. However, some – like the fighters and bombers – are of course combat aircraft which nevertheless can be seen at some overseas airports. It is not uncommon for military and civil aircraft to share the same airfield and perhaps some of the aircraft detailed here may be glimpsed from the window of an airliner.

A word of caution: most military authorities are sensitive about aircraft spotters and care should be taken to avoid breaking local laws. Even the most innocent act might be misunderstood, so take care when you use a camera!

As in the previous chapter, for the most part metric measurements have been used except where imperial measures are more commonly employed. The types are listed alphabetically, regardless of nationality or of rôle.

Helicopters have revolutionised air
warfare by enabling troops and guns to
be moved about the battlefield.

Aeritalia G.222 Length 22·7m Wing span 28·8m Height 9·8m Range 2,950km Max. take-off weight 26,500 kg Max. speed 540km/h (336mph) Accommodation 44 troops Power plant 2 × General Electric T64 turboprops of 3,400shp or 2 × Rolls-Royce Tyne turboprops of 6,106ehp A tactical transport aircraft, the G.222 can also carry 32 paratroops or cargo. Electronic-counter-measures and maritime patrol versions are projected.

Aerospatiale Frégate Length 19·28m Wing span 22·60m Height 6·21m Range 1,450km Max. take-off weight 10,800kg Max. cruising speed 408km/h (254mph) Accommodation 26 passengers Power plant 2 × Turbomeca Bastan VII turboprops of 1,145ehp This passenger or cargo transport is in service with the French and other air forces.

Aermacchi MB.326 Length 10·64m Wing span 10·85m Height 3·72m Range 1,850km Armament 6 underwing hardpoints for bombs, rockets, fuel tanks, gun pods etc. Max. speed 867km/h (539mph) Power plant 1 Rolls-Royce Viper turbojet of 3,750lb thrust A popular Italian trainer/ground attack design used by many air forces and licence-built in several countries.

Aerospatiale Alouette II Length 9·75m Rotor diameter 10·20m Height 2·75m Range 100km Max. take-off weight 1,650kg Max. cruising speed 205km/h (127mph) Accommodatipn 5 seats Power plant 1 Turbomeca Artouste II turboshaft of 360shp Over 1,000 of these versatile helicopters have been built. They are in service with the forces of many countries. The larger 7-seat Alouette III has also been produced in large numbers.

Aero L-29 Delfin Length: 10·81m Wing span 10·29m Height 3·13m Range 640km Armament 2 underwing hardpoints for gun pods, fuel tanks or small bombs. Max. speed 655km/h (407mph) Power plant 1 M-701 turbojet of 1,960lb thrust This Czechoslovakian design became the standard trainer of the Eastern bloc and has been adopted by some other air forces, particularly in Africa.

Aerospatiale/Westland Gazelle Length 11·97m Rotor diameter 10·50m Height 3·15m Range 360km Accommodation 5 seats Max. cruising speed 264km/h (164mph) Max. take-off weight 1,800kg Produced in large numbers, this helicopter can be used to carry anti-tank missiles, rockets or machine guns.

Aerospatiale/Westland Puma

Length 18·15m Rotor diameter 15·00m Height 5·14m Range 572km Max. take-off weight 7,000kg Max. cruising speed 257km/h (159mph) Accommodation 16 troops or cargo Power plant 2 × Turbomeca Turmo turboshaft of 1,328shp This tactical helicopter is operated by many air forces. Missiles, cannon or machine-guns can be carried.

Antonov An-12 (NATO Code-name 'CUB')

Length 33·10m Wing span 38·00m Height 10·53m Range 3,600km Max. take-off weight 61,000kg Max. cruising speed 600km/h (373mph) Accommodation 100 paratroops or cargo Power plant 4 × Ivchenko AI-20K turboprops of 4,000ehp Armament 2 × 23mm cannon in the tail Produced in large numbers for the Soviet air force as well as for other countries, this transport aircraft can land on grass strips.

Aerospatiale (Potez/Fouga) Magister

Length 10·06m Wing span 11·4m Height 2·80m Range 1,250km Armament 2 × machine-guns and 2 underwing hardpoints for bombs, rockets or missiles Max. speed 650km/h (403mph) Power plant 2 × Turbomeca Marboré turbojets of 880lbs thrust Distinctive for its butterfly tail, this trainer is also used for ground attack duties.

Bell 204 UH-1 Iroquois

Length 16·15m Rotor diameter 13·41m Height 4·39m Range 400km/h Max. take-off weight 2,631kg Max. speed 204 km/h (127mph) Accommodation up to 10 seats Power plant 1 Lycoming T.53 turboshaft of 640shp The model 204 was the father of the 'Huey' family which was produced in very large numbers. Over 70 countries operate various versions including marine helicopters which can carry torpedoes.

Antonov An-2 (NATO Code-name 'COLT')

Length 12·74m Wing span 18·18m Height 4·00m Range 900km Max. take-off weight 5,500kg Max. cruising speed 258km/h (160mph) Accommodation 12 passengers Power plant 1 Shvestov ASh-62IR piston engine of 1,000hp Over 10,000 of these bi-plane transports have been built and are in service with the air forces of some 44 countries.

Breguet Atlantic

Length 31·75m Wing span 36·3m Height 11·33m Range 9,000km Max. take-off weight 43,500kg Max. speed 658km/h (409mph) Armament bombs, depth charges, torpedoes Underwing hardpoints for missiles. Power plant 2 × Rolls-Royce Tyne 21 turboprops of 6,106ehp Used by several NATO forces as well as Pakistan, this maritime patrol aircraft is being developed into a higher-performance version.

British Aerospace (Hawker Siddeley) Harrier Length 13·87m Wing span 7·70m Max. take-off weight 9,752kg Cruising speed 1,186km/h (737mph) Range 640km Accommodation 1 pilot Power plant 1 Rolls-Royce Pegasus 103 of 21,500lbs thrust. The world's first vertical take-off combat aircraft the Harrier is in service with several armed forces, and the Sea Harrier has been developed for shipboard service.

BAC (English Electric) Canberra Length 19·96m Wing span 19·50m Height 4·72m Range 4828km Max. speed 1,040km/h (620mph) Power plant 2 × Rolls-Royce RA3 Avon turbojets of 6,500lb thrust This thirty-year-old design has become a classic and remains in service with a number of air forces as a bomber and reconnaissance aircraft.

British Aerospace (Hawker Siddeley) Hawk Length 11·95m Wing span 9·4m Height 4·09m Range 1,207km Max. take-off weight 7,375kg Max. speed 1,014km/h (630mph) Armament 5 hardpoints to carry 30mm cannon, bombs or rockets Power plant 1 Rolls-Royce/Turbomeca Adour 151 turbofan of 5,340lb thrust A new generation trainer/ground attack aircraft which will see service in Europe, Africa and the Far East.

BAC (Hunting) Jet Provost/ Strikemaster Length 10·27m Wing span 11·23m Height 3·34m Range 1,166km Max. speed 774km/h (481mph) Max. take-off weight 5,210kg Armament (Strikemaster) 2 × 7·62mm machine guns, rockets or bombs on eight underwing hardpoints Power plant 1 Rolls-Royce Viper 535 turbojet of 3,410lb thrust Originally developed from the Percival Provost piston-engined trainer, the Jet Provost and its ground attack variant have been adopted by many air forces.

British Aerospace (Scottish Aviation) Bulldog Length 7·09m Wing span 10·06m Height 2·28m Accommodation 2 seats Max. speed 241km/h (150mph) Power plant 1 Lycoming IO-360 piston engine of 200hp This primary trainer is in use by a number of air forces and can carry machine-guns, rockets or missiles.

Cessna T-37/A-37 Length 8·92m Wing span: 10·93m Height 2·7m Range 740km Max. take-off weight 6,350kg Max. speed 816km/h (507mph) Armament 1 machine-gun in the nose and eight underwing hardpoints to carry bombs, rockets etc. Power plant 2 × General Electric J85-17A turbojets of 2,850lb thrust Another 'first-generation' trainer/ground attack aircraft which is still in widespread use in several countries.

Dassault Breguet (Dornier) Alpha Jet
Length 12·29m Wing span 9·12m Max. take-off weight 7,000kg Max. cruising speed 900km/h (560mph) Range 2,430km Accommodation 2 crew Power plant 2 SNECMA/Turbomeca Larzac 04 two-shaft turbo-fans of 2,976lbs thrust. Trainer aircraft capable of undertaking combat missions.

Dassault Mirage IIIC
Length 14·77m Wing span 8·22m Height 4·25m Range 1,200km Max. speed 2,300km/h (1,430mph) Power plant: 1 SNECMA Atar 9B turbojet of 13,225lb thrust One of the most successful jet fighters so far produced, this aircraft is the first-line defence of many countries.

de Havilland Canada Caribou
Length 22·13m Wing span 29·15m Height 9·7m Range 390km Max. take-off weight 14,197kg Max. speed 347km/h (216mph) Accommodation 32 troops or cargo Power plant: 2 × Pratt & Whitney R-2000 piston engines of 1,450hp Over 300 of this STOL tactical transport aircraft have been produced and many remain in service.

de Havilland Canada Buffalo
Length 24·08m Wing span 29·26m Height 8·73m Range 815km Max. take-off weight 22,316kg Max. speed 420km/h (261mph) Accommodation 41 troops or cargo Power plant 2 × General Electric T-64 turboprops of 3,133shp Clearly developed from the Caribou, the Buffalo features a general all-round improvement in performance. It has an excellent STOL capability.

Fairchild C119 Packet
Length 26·36m Wing span 34·3m Height 8·07m Range 1,595km Max. take-off weight 33,600kg Max. speed 402km/h (250mph) Accommodation bulky cargo Power plant 2 × Wright R-3350 piston engines of 3,350hp Although production of this transport aircraft ended over 25 years ago, a number remain in the service of air forces in several countries.

General Dynamics F-111
Length 22·4m Wing span 9·74m Max. take-off weight 44,906kg Max. cruising speed 2,335km/h (1,450mph) Range 5,093km Accommodation 2 crew Power plant 2 Pratt & Whitney RF30 two-shaft afterburning turbofans of 25,100lbs thrust. Developed to meet all future tactical needs of all the US services, and a number of variants are available.

General Dynamics F-16 Length 14·52m Wing span 9·45m Height 5·01m Range 2,100km Max. speed 2,090km/h (1,300mph) Armament 1 20mm cannon, 9 hardpoints for carrying missiles, rockets, bombs or fuel tanks. Power plant 1 Pratt & Whitney F-100 turbofan of 24,000lb thrust The victor of a hard-fought battle for orders from NATO countries, the F-16 will replace ageing F-104 Starfighters.

Hawker Siddeley Nimrod Length 38·63m Wing span 35·00m Height 9·08m Range 8,340km Max. speed 926km/h (575mph) Armament torpedoes, mines, depth charges in the weapons bay and provision for missiles underwing. Power plant 4 × Rolls-Royce Spey 250 turbofans of 12,140lb thrust Based on the Comet civil transport this maritime reconnaissance aircraft can remain airborne for 12 hours and is an effective submarine killer.

Grumman Tracker Length: 12·88m Wing span 21·23m Height 4·96m Range 1,448km Max. speed 462km/h (287mph) Armament torpedoes, depth charges in weapons bay. 6 underwing hardpoints for bombs, rockets etc. Power plant 2 × Wright Cyclone piston engines of 1,525hp A 25-year old design, the Tracker is still operating as a patrol/anti-submarine aircraft for over a dozen nations.

Hawker Siddeley (Folland) Gnat Length 9·65m Wing span 7·32m Height 3·2m Range 1,900km Max. speed 1,026km/h (636mph) Armament 4 underwing hardpoints for fuel tanks or bombs Power plant 1 Bristol-Siddeley-Orpheus 101 turbojet of 4,230lb thrust An advanced trainer made famous by the RAF's Red Arrows formation aerobatic team.

Hawker Hunter Length 13·98m Wing span 10·26m Height 4·26m Range 850km Max. speed 1,144km/h (710mph) Armament 4 × 30mm cannon. 4 underwing hardpoints for bombs, missiles or fuel tanks. Power plant: 1 Rolls-Royce Avon turbojet of 10,150lb thrust A very popular fighter/ground attack aircraft which is still in widespread use.

Ilyushin Il-28 (NATO Code-name 'BEAGLE') Length 17·65m Wing span 21·45m Height 6·7m Range 1,100km Max. speed 900km/h (559mph) Armament 2 × 23mm cannon in the nose, plus 2 in the tail. Bombs in the weapons bay or on underwing hardpoints. Power plant 2 × Klimov VK-1 turbojets of 5,952lb thrust This early-vintage light bomber is still being used by many air forces.

IAI Arava Length 13·03m Wing span 20·96m Height 5·21m Range 500km Max. take-off weight: 6,803kg Max. speed: 326km/h (203mph) Accommodation 24 troops or cargo Power plant 2 × Pratt & Whitney Canada PT6A-34 turboprops of 750shp This Israeli-designed military transport is in service with several Latin American air forces.

Lockheed Hercules Length 29·78m Wing span 40·41m Height 11·66m Range 4,002km Max. take-off weight 79,380kg Max. speed 618km/h (384mph) Accommodation 92 troops or cargo Power plant 4 × Allison T.56 turbo-props of 3,750ehp First flown in 1954, this versatile transport is still in production to meet a continuing demand. Some 40 air forces operate the type.

IAI Kfir Length 16·5m Wing span 8·22m Max. take-off weight 14,600kg Max. speed 2,495km (1,550mph) Range 1,125km Accommodation 1 pilot Power plant 1 General Electric J79-17 single-shaft turbo-jet with afterburner. A multi-role fighter bomber built by Israel Aircraft Industries.

Lockheed Starfighter Length 16·69m Wing span 6·68m Height 4·11m Range 483km Max. speed 2,330km/h (1,450mph) Armament various missiles on underwing or wing-tip hardpoints Bombs or rockets can also be carried Power plant 1 General Electric J.79 turbojet of 14,800lb thrust Over 1,000 of this needle-nosed fighter were built; many remain in use with NATO and other forces.

Lockheed T-33 Length 11·48m Wing span 11·85m Height 3·55m Range 2,165km Max. speed 950km/h (590mph) Armament not normally armed but can carry bombs Power plant 1 Allison J33 turbojet of 5,200lb thrust Many examples of this jet trainer – the world's first – are still in service. The pleasing lines belie its vintage!

Lockheed Starlifter Length 44·2m Wing span 48·74m Height 11·96m Range 6,565km Max. take-off weight 143,600kg Max speed 919km/h (571mph) Accommodation 154 troops or cargo Power plant 4 × Pratt & Whitney TF.33 turbofans of 21,000lb thrust The mainstay of the USAF Military Airlift Command, each of the Starlifter fleet is to be stretched by 7.11m.

Lockheed Orion Length 35·61m Wing span 30·37m Height 10·29m Range 7,725km Max. speed 761km/h (473mph) Armament torpedoes, depth charges or mines in the weapons bay Rockets or anti-submarine missiles under the wing Power plant 4 × Allison T.56 turboprops of 4,500ehp Produced in large numbers, this maritime reconnaissance/anti-submarine aircraft was developed from the Electra airliner.

Lockheed Galaxy Length 75·54m Wing span 67·88m Height 19·85m Range 6,033km Max. take-off weight 348,810kg Max. speed 919km/h (571mph) Accommodation 345 troops — more usually bulky cargo such as tanks etc. Power plant 4 × General Electric TF39 turbofans of 41,000lb thrust The world's largest aircraft, the C-5A was designed as a strategic freighter for the US Military Airlift Command.

McDonnell Douglas F15 Eagle Length 19·43m Wing span 13·05m Max. take-off weight 25,401kg Cruising speed 3,057km/h (1,900mph) Range 4,631km Accommodation 1 pilot Power plant 2 Pratt & Whitney F100 turbofans of 25,000lbs thrust. A high performance interceptor fighter which can also be used in the ground attack role.

McDonnell-Douglas Phantom II Length 17·76m Wing span 11·70m Height 4·96m Range approx. 1,450km Max. speed 2,414km/h (1,500mph) Armament 1 20mm cannon, various air-to-air missiles Bombs, missiles, etc can be carried on 4 underwing and one under-fuselage hardpoints Power plant 2 × General Electric J.79 turbojets of 17,000lb thrust (RAF aircraft are fitted with Rolls-Royce Speys) The most successful and widely-used fighter in current use by a dozen forces.

MiG-17 (NATO Code-name 'FRESCO') Length 11·05m Wing span 9.45m Height 3·35m Range approx. 1,470km Max. speed 1,145km/h (711mph) Armament 3 × 23mm cannon 4 underwing hardpoints for bombs, rockets or missiles Power plant 1 Klimov turbojet of 5,952lb thrust Of the 5,000 or so built, some of these fighters remain in service, mainly with East European and 'third world' countries.

MiG-21 (NATO Code-name 'FISHBED') Length: 14·6m Wing span 7.15m Height 4·5m Range 1,100km Max. speed 2,070km/h (1,285mph) Armament 2 × 30mm cannon. 4 underwing hardpoints for missiles or rockets Power plant 1 Tumansky turbojet of 11,240lb thrust Adopted by several air forces as an all-weather fighter, the delta-winged MiG-21 can carry bombs for ground attack duties.

Mig-25 (NATO Code-name 'FOXBAT') Length 21m
Wing span 12·2m Max. take-off weight 37,194 kg Cruising speed 3,050km/h (1,900mph) Range 1,130km Accommodation 1 pilot Power plant 2 Tumansky R-266 turbo-jets of 27,000lbs thrust with after-burning. The leading Soviet high performance interceptor, which also serves as a reconnaissance aircraft.

North American Sabre Length 11·43m Wing span 11·31m Height 4·47m Range 1,368km Max. speed 1,091km/h (678mph) Armament 6 × 12mm machine guns underwing hardpoints for bombs, rockets or missiles Power plant 1 General Electric J47 turbojet of 5,800lb thrust Few of the over 9,000 built remain in service but some air forces still operate this veteran fighter.

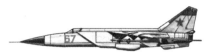

Mil Mi-4 (NATO Code-name 'HOUND') Length 16·80m Rotor diameter 21·00m Height 5·18m Range 400km Max. take-off weight 7,800kg Cruising speed 160km/h (99mph) Accommodation 14 troops or cargo Power plant 1 Shvetsov ASh-82V piston engine of 1,700hp Supplied to many Eastern bloc and other air forces as a general-purpose helicopter.

Northrop F5 Freedom Fighter Length 14·38m Wing span 7·7m Height 4·01m Range 2,232km Max. speed 1,489km/h (925mph) Armament 2 × 20mm cannon and 5 hardpoints for missiles, rockets, fuel tanks, etc. Power plant 2 × General Electric J.85 turbo-jets of 4,080lb thrust Developed as a private venture from the Talon supersonic trainer the Freedom Fighter and later Tiger II have been built in large numbers.

Mil Mi-8 (NATO Code-name 'HIP')
Length 25·24m Rotor diameter 21·29m Height 5·65m Range 480km Max. take-off weight 12,000kg Max. speed 260km/h (161mph) Armament can be fitted with gun-pods, rockets or anti-tank missiles. Accommodation 24 troops or cargo Power plant 2 × Isotov turboshafts of 1,500shp More then 1,000 of these transport helicopters have been built and some 23 air forces are equipped with them.

Panavia Tornado Length 16·7m Wing span 13·9m spread, 8.6m swept Max. take-off weight 24,000kg Cruising speed 2,125km/h (1,320mph) Range 1,250km Accommodation 2 crew Power plant 2 Turbo-Union RB 199 turbo-fans of 1,5000lbs thrust with after-burning. A multi-role aircraft built by a consortium of three countries – Italy, Germany and Britain – it is notable for its variable geometry wing.

Pilatus Turbo-Porter Length 11·23m Wing span 15·14m Height 3.73, Range 898km Max. take-off weight 2,767kg Max. cruising speed 262km/h (163mph) Accommodation 10 seats or cargo Power plant 1 Pratt & Whitney Canada PT6A-27 turboprop of 550shp The exceptional STOL performance of this Swiss design has attracted orders from forces in many parts of the world.

Shorts Skyvan Length 12·60m Wing span 19·79m Height 4·60m Range 1,075km Max. take-off weight 6,214kg Max. cruising speed 327km/h (203mph) Accommodation 22 troops or cargo Power plant 2 × Garrett TPE331 turboprops of 715shp A STOL light transport which is in service in many parts of the world.

Saab Scania AJ37 Viggen Length 16·43m Wing span 10·60m Max. take-off weight 22,500kg Cruising speed 2,180km/h (1,350mph) Range 1,000km Accommodation 1 pilot Power plant 1 Volvo Flygmotor RM 8A turbo-fan of 26,000lbs thrust with after-burner. This is a delta-winged strike aircraft, which is being developed into the JA37 Interceptor version.

SIAI/Marchetti SF260 Length 7·10m Wing span 8·25m Height 2·41m Range 1,490km Max. speed 340km/h (211mph) Armament 2 underwing hardpoints for bombs, machine gun pods, rockets etc. Power plant 1 Lycoming O-540 piston engine of 260hp Large numbers of this Italian trainer have been sold. It can also be used for counter-insurgency operations.

Sepecat Jaguar Length 15·52m Wing span 8·69m Max. take-off weight 14,968kg Cruising speed 1,600km/h (1,050mph) Range 800km Accommodation 1 pilot Power plant 2 × Rolls-Royce/Turbomeca Adour Mark 102 turbo-fans of 7,380lbs thrust with after-burner. A joint development by Britain and France to fill the training and attack roles.

Sikorsky S-65 Length 26·9m Rotor diameter 22·02m Height 7·6m Range 869km Max. take-off weight 19,050kg Max. speed 315km/h (196mph) Accommodation 55 troops or cargo Power plant 2 × General Electric T.64 of 2,850shp The largest Western heavy transport helicopter, the CH-53, as it is known in its military designation, can also be used as a mine-sweeper.

Sikorsky S-70 Length 19·76m Rotor diameter 16·36m Height 5·00m Max. take-off weight 9,707kg Max. speed 318km/h (198mph) Accommodation 11 troops or cargo Power plant 2 × General Electric T.700 turboshafts of 1,536shp Winner of the UTTAS (Utility Tactical Transport Aircraft System) competition held by the US Army, the UH-60A will be produced in large numbers.

Transall C-160 Length 32·40m Wing span 40·00m Height 12·36m Range 1,700km Max. take-off weight 51,000kg Max. speed 592km/h (368mph) Accommodation 93 troops or cargo Power plant 2 × Rolls-Royce Tyne turboprops of 6,100ehp Produced for the French and German air forces, this transport is also in service with the Turkish and South African air forces.

Sukhoi Su-7 (NATO Code-name 'FITTER') Length 17·37m Wing span 8·93m Height 4·70m Max. speed 1,700km/h (1,055mph) Armament 2 × 30mm cannon and 4 underwing hardpoints to carry bombs, missiles, etc. Power plant 1 Lyulka AL-7F turbojet of 15,430lb thrust A ground-attack fighter supplied to several 'third world' countries as well as the Eastern bloc.

Westland (Saro) Scout Length 12·29m Rotor diameter 9·83m Height 3·56m Range 510km Max. speed 211km/h (131mph) Accommodation 4 seats Armament anti-tank guided weapons or rocket pods Power plant 1 Bristol Siddeley Nimbus turboshaft of 685shp A tactical helicopter which can be used to attack tanks as well as to transport personnel.

Sukhoi Su-15 (NATO Code-name 'FLAGON') Length 20·5m Wing span 9·15m Max. take-off weight 20,412kg Cruising speed 2,180km/h (1,350mph) Range 725km Accommodation 1 pilot Power plant 2 Tumansky R25 turbo-jets of 16,500lbs thrust with after-burner. This is the standard interceptor of the Soviet Air Force. Many of the aircraft in service are of the latest D, E and F variants.

Westland/Aerospatiale Lynx Length 15·16m Rotor diameter 12·80m Height 3·66m Range 761m Max. take-off weight 4196kg Max. speed 333km/h (207mph) Accommodation 10 troops or cargo Armament anti-tank missiles or rocket and machine-gun pods Power plant 2 × Rolls-Royce Gem turboshafts of 900shp Produced in army and marine versions, the Lynx will replace the Scout helicopter.

Whirling wings

Records show that over a thousand years ago a popular toy with Chinese children was a couple of feathers fixed to a stick. The little device rose into the sky like a flying top when spun vigorously. Doubtless for years scientists also pondered the 'flying' qualities of the spinning seeds of the sycamore tree but it took a long time before the mechanical problems of getting rotating wings to rise vertically into the air could be overcome.

As with conventional fixed-wing aircraft, many inventors understood the potential of spinning wings or rotors to lift men into the sky. Once more the names of Leonardo da Vinci and Sir George Cayley are linked with the earliest experiments and designs in rotary flight but the lack of a suitable motor prevented the practical fulfillment of their ideas.

Leonardo da Vinci tried to design a helicopter in the sixteenth century.

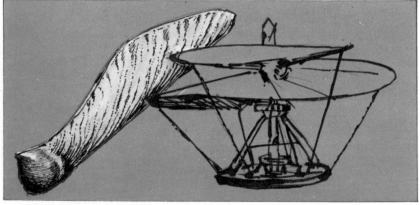

Many scientists had a vivid imagination but were still unsuccessful!

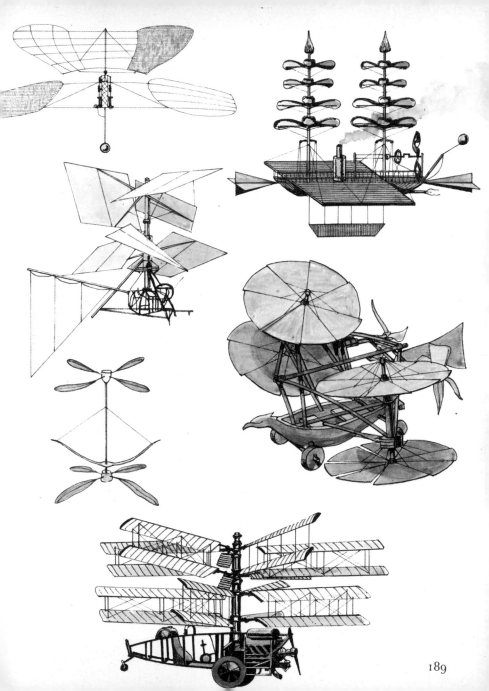

In 1863 the Vicomte Gustave de Ponton d'Amecourt and a band of rotary-wing enthusiasts made a steam-powered model. He called it a hélicoptère from the Greek *helicos* (spiral) and *pteron* (wing). As we have learned in our opening chapter, aircraft development had to await the advent of the piston engine before the dreams of scientists could be realised. To France, always a pioneer in the science of aviation, goes the honour of the first successes in vertical flight. In 1907 the Breguet brothers teamed with Charles Richet to produce a strange-looking craft which did manage to rise about one metre into the air. It was another Frenchman, however, Paul Cornu, who produced the first man-carrying helicopter although this too did not reach a great height.

The first commercially successful rotary-winged aircraft was the autogiro designed by a Spaniard – Juan de la Cierva. He overcame the problem of driving the rotor by allowing it to rotate freely in the air. Forward propulsion was achieved by a conventional propeller in the nose of the aircraft and as the rotor spun it lifted the aircraft into the air. An autogiro cannot hover, but Cierva later devised a means of spinning the rotor on the ground so that the pilot could make the aircraft 'jump' into the air. Several hundred autogiros were built but the notion of an aircraft capable of hovering still tempted designers to solve the problems of the helicopter. Sir George Cayley produced plans for a twin-rotor design and in 1937 Dr Heinrich Focke built the Focke-Achgelis Fa-61 based on the same principle. The machine proved to have such excellent handling qualities that it was dramatically demonstrated inside a covered sports stadium in Berlin. Although the twin rotor layout adopted by these early pioneers avoided the problems of torque, it was usually at the cost of the payload.

Some extraordinary devices were built — and remained firmly on the ground. Vertical flight was not easy.

The first successful rotary-winged aircraft was the autogiro designed by Juan de la Cierva.

The advent of World War Two proved to be both a stimulus and a hindrance in the development of the helicopter. Some pioneer designers had to put aside their plans for helicopters to concentrate on the construction of conventional warplanes. In America, however, Igor Sikorsky resumed experiments which he had begun in Russia in 1909. His early ventures were not a success and – like the Breguet brothers – he turned to the design of fixed-wing aircraft. In 1939, however, he flew his VS-300 which had a single main rotor and a small tail rotor – a pattern which has been copied in most designs ever since. The function of the tail rotor is to counteract torque – a phenomenon which produces a reaction to the spinning of the rotor drive shaft. Without the tail rotor, the body of the helicopter would spin in the opposite direction to that of the main rotor. Sikorsky's single-rotor design needed only one engine, allowing a saving in weight so that passengers could be carried. The armed forces of several nations could see the

Helicopters have developed from single-seat designs (*inset*) to sophisticated types such as the Westland Sea King.

192

potential of the helicopter and Sikorsky was encouraged to put his designs into production. The Royal Navy was an early enthusiast for the helicopter, ordering the Sikorsky R.5 for anti-submarine patrol duties. Later development of the helicopter often depended upon the demands brought about by warfare. The Korean War boosted the use of the helicopter as a means of rescue; hundreds of 'downed' pilots were picked up from the sea or snatched from behind enemy lines by daring 'chopper' crews. Wounded soldiers were also carried swiftly to medical aid by helicopters – sometimes the only means of transport capable of reaching remote areas.

The Vietnam War was to provide another boost in the popularity of the helicopter. For army commanders realised that if remote areas could be reached to evacuate wounded men, helicopters could also be used to lift troops *into* enemy territory. Consequently thousands more helicopters were produced to transport personnel, weapons and supplies to the front line. The ability of helicopters to manoeuvre close to the ground led to another new use – forward air control. Helicopter crews could direct the fire of artillery or fighter-bombers on to targets which could best be identified at close range. Finally, armed helicopters were produced to attack armoured vehicles – rotary-winged aircraft had been developed for an aggressive role as fixed-wing aircraft had before them. The jet age brought about a revolution in helicopter performance which was not as obviously apparent as in conventional aircraft. The smooth running gas turbines helped to reduce the vibration and noise usually associated with helicopters; the speed and lifting capacity of turbine-powered helicopters was increased too.

It may be wondered quite why the helicopter has been an aircraft used mainly by the armed forces. It is simply a matter of cost. Its complex mechanism is expensive both to produce and to maintain, making the helicopter less economical than fixed-wing aircraft. However its ability to hover, fly backwards, sideways or forwards puts it at an advantage over conventional aircraft for many special tasks, both civil and military. A close look at just how a helicopter flies will explain why this unique form of transport is basically more complex than an aeroplane.

The main rotor (figure 1) is essentially a wing which, you will remember, provides lift when pushed through the air at sufficient speed. Unfortunately the whirling wing of a helicopter is somewhat more complicated than a fixed wing. We shall see that it is necessary for it to flap up and down, alter its angle of incidence and bend at the hub. The main rotor also serves as a 'propeller' which, when tilted, will pull the helicopter in the required direction.

It was Cierva who made important discoveries regarding rotary-winged flight. Those who had earlier studied helicopter design had assumed that the powered wings or 'blades' of the rotor had to be set at a high angle of attack to gain lift. Cierva found, on the contrary, that by setting the blades at a very low angle of attack a whirling rotor would provide sufficient lift to sustain flight without power. Auto-rotation was the name given to this phenomenon and all modern helicopters are capable of flying in this way should an engine fail. Cierva's blades were set at such an angle that they would not begin spinning in the airstream but once set in motion

they would revolve automatically even when there was no forward power. The Spaniard devised a method of spinning the rotor on the ground by a mechanical drive from the engine. As soon as the required speed was attained, the transmission was declutched and the propeller in the nose pulled the autogiro through the air. The aircraft could fly at very low speeds and even if the engine failed, the rotor continued to turn as the airflow from below kept the blades moving; the autogiro could descend as if on a parachute (figure 2). Cierva's careful design ensured that even when the craft was descending the whirling rotors gained lift both from their own motion and from the upward flow of air; his autogiro could land as gently as a spinning sycamore seed.

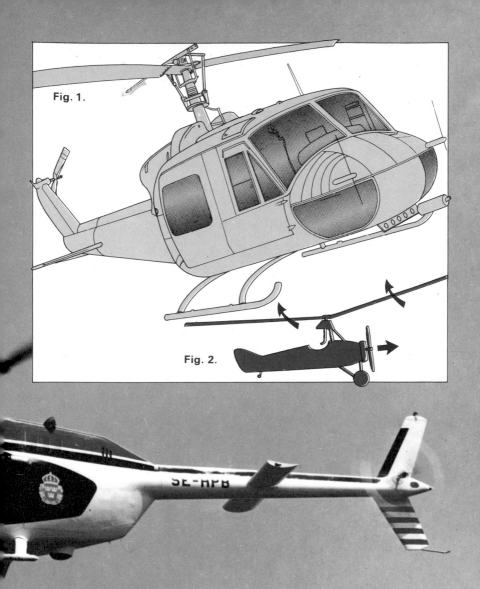

Fig. 1.

Fig. 2.

Many police forces use helicopters for traffic control and other duties. A Swedish Agusta-Bell Jet Ranger is seen in flight.

Cierva discovered another important aspect of rotary-winged flight – the need for the blades to 'flap'. It should be noted that as an autogiro or helicopter moves forward, the advancing blades will move faster than a retreating blade (figure 3). The faster-moving advancing blade will therefore produce more lift and if unchecked will tip the aircraft over. Indeed, it was just such an accident that led Cierva to encounter this problem. His solution was the flapping blade; as it advanced, adding its own speed to that of the forward movement of the aircraft, the hinge at the hub allowed the blade to rise instead of tipping the machine over. This discovery too has benefited helicopter design and present-day machines incorporate flapping rotor-blades (figure 4). (On some 'rigid-rotor' helicopters the hinge has been eliminated but the flexible attachment to the hub achieves the same effect.) As the blade retreats, the forward speed of the machine is lost and the hinge allows it to go down with the decrease of lift. The result is a balanced lift and a level fuselage.

If you study the rotor head of any present-day helicopter you will see that it is a complicated mechanism. For in addition to the hinge which allows the blade to flap, there is another one which enables the blades to drag. We have seen that advancing blades move faster than retreating ones; to encounter the tendency of the blades to bend in these circumstances (for, of course, they slow down as they retreat) a hinge allows some movement at the hub (figure 5).

There are still more control devices at the hub, however: when the pilot wants to change the direction of flight, he banks the helicopter just like an aeroplane but, as he lacks ailerons, some other means of manoeuvring must be found. A control column is moved in much the same way as that of a fixed-wing aircraft. This is called the cyclic pitch lever; in order to tilt the helicopter the pitch of the blades is increased at one point in their cycle of rotation. If by changing the pitch at one particular point or cyclically the helicopter can be steered, it follows that by changing the pitch of the blades uniformly (or collectively) the helicopter can be made to rise or fall. By increasing the angle of attack of all the blades together the lift generated will be increased as well. In aeronautics any gain is usually offset by a loss, and the extra lift generated by the increase in pitch is accompanied by an increase in drag. Extra power is therefore needed to climb. The pilot has a collective pitch lever which controls the climb and descent of the helicopter. A swash plate on the rotor hub conducts the pilot's instructions to the rotor blades, increasing the pitch collectively or cyclically as required. As the collective pitch is pulled up and the helicopter rises, extra power is automatically pro-

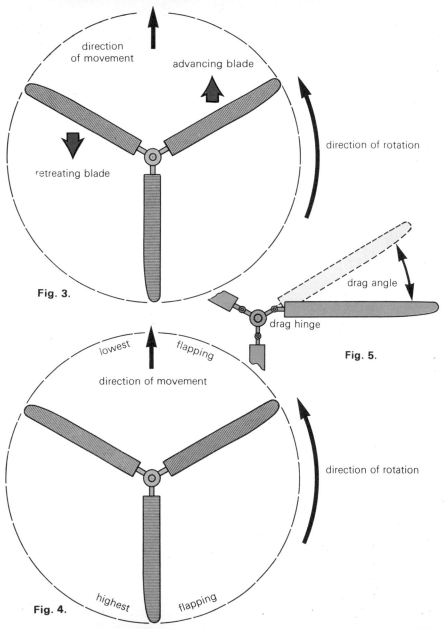

direction
of movement

advancing blade

direction of rotation

retreating blade

Fig. 3.

drag angle

drag hinge

Fig. 5.

lowest   flapping

direction of movement

direction of rotation

highest   flapping

Fig. 4.

Inset above Only a helicopter is capable of hovering over difficult terrain.

Below Helicopters have proved to be invaluable at sea.

vided by the engine but a twist grip throttle (rather like that on a motor bike) is used for fine adjustments of power. The pilot also has rudder pedals but instead of a rudder he can swing the tail around by altering the pitch of the tail rotor blades (figure 6). By increasing the pitch the tail rotor will try to 'climb' or, in this case, pull the tail around. Conversely if the pitch is reduced torque will turn the fuselage in the opposite direction.

Fig. 6. Altering the pitch of the tail rotor blades.

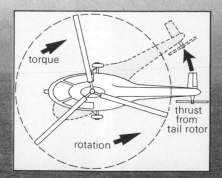

Flying a helicopter calls for precise skills on the part of the pilot, not unlike those of trying to balance a soup plate on a knitting needle! It is easy to 'over-control' the machine by setting up a pendulum motion, as each error leads to another. Hovering calls for the greatest concentration as the pilot must counter the effects of wind drift as well as keeping the 'soup plate' balanced. You may notice that helicopters rarely hover in fact, for it is very demanding in terms of power and therefore fuel consumption. If you watch a helicopter take off or land it only hovers momentarily close to the ground, usually adopting a markedly tilted attitude as it flies on its way.

As a means of transport to such remote places as off-shore oil rigs and lighthouses, a unique way of saving shipwrecked sailors, or simply as the most direct way of getting from point to point where no runway is available, the helicopter is without equal.

Flights of fancy~a look into the future

In a little over 75 years, aviation has progressed astonishingly. Every day passengers are flown in comfort at speeds faster than a bullet as the graceful Concorde streaks across the sky and hundreds of passengers fly in jumbo-sized airliners with the unconcern of commuters travelling by train. Surely few can doubt that the next 75 years will witness giant strides in air travel.

There are many influences which will shape the airliners of tomorrow, the skill of aircraft and engine designers being only one. Experts differ as to how long the world's oil resources will last but it is obvious that other fuels will have to be used eventually. Atomic reactors may ultimately provide the necessary power to propel the airliners of the future although some have great doubts about the safety of nuclear-powered aircraft.

Liquid hydrogen is a more likely candidate to replace kerosene in the next decade or so. Much lighter than oil-based fuels, liquid hydrogen does, however, present some problems in that it must be stored at $-253°C$. Another problem to challenge the design team is that liquid hydrogen has a very low density, having some four times the volume of kerosene of the equivalent energy. Despite these difficulties, studies are being carried out which could lead to hydrogen-fuelled airliners before the end of the century.

For the next 25 years or so kerosene and petrol are likely to remain the principal sources of power for aircraft. Only a tiny percentage of the world's oil production is used by aviation but the steady increase in fuel costs provides a constant stimulus to designers to improve the efficiency of airliners. Computers, new materials, and refinements of present designs will all contribute to better airliners of tomorrow.

Already computers are being used to 'manage' the fuel during an airliner's journey, automatically adjusting the throttles to make sure that none is wasted. Another computer makes sure that navigation is highly accurate and avoids unnecessary kilometres. Yet another computer will be an integral part of 'control configured' aircraft. This eliminates unnecessary control movements, resulting in a saving in fuel and a reduction in the size of the control surfaces. Lockheed have already planned 'control configured' versions of the TriStar.

The use of plastic and carbon-fibre materials will make for lighter and therefore more fuel-efficient aircraft. New materials in engine

Above Concorde — the only successful supersonic airliner in service today.

Below This is how Lockheed envisage hydrogen-fuelled airliners.

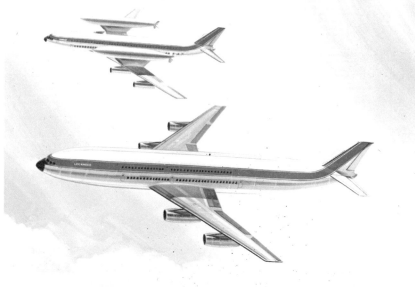

Hypersonic airliners capable of nearly 9,200 k.p.h. may one day fly beyond the stratosphere.

construction will also make for jets which will burn less fuel. It is possible that turboprop engines will make a come-back, for research has shown that special propellers can reduce flying costs considerably. Curved blades of a new design are said to be more efficient than conventional propellers and by the end of this decade the 'prop-fan', as it is called, may be putting theories into practice.

Advances in aerodynamics have made possible some improvements in performance. One such is the 'super-critical' wing which has been adopted by many modern designs.

You will remember that the air flows more quickly over the top of a wing than it does at the bottom. (Disturbed by the camber, it hurries to rejoin the less disturbed flow from beneath.) It follows that at high sub-sonic speeds the airflow over the upper wing surface will reach 'critical' super-sonic speeds before the rest of the airflow. By careful design it is possible to delay the onset of this critical over-wing airflow. Super-critical wings, therefore, are being employed on aircraft of all sizes from a planned Light Transport Aircraft under development by Dornier to the A.310 airliner manufactured by Airbus, the consortium formed by European governments.

Wing-tip winglets also improve performance by reducing the turbulence set up by vortices (air from the upper wing trying to mix with that from below). A feature of the latest Learjets and the Arava transport aircraft, 'winglets' will be adopted for more designs in the future.

Airliners are so expensive to develop that they have to have a long production life if the manufacturers are to recover their invest-ment. Airlines, too, prefer to buy aircraft which seem certain to enjoy a long and productive life. A 20-year production run is by no means uncommon so we can be pretty certain that the Boeing 747, 757 and 767 are likely to be coming off the production lines in the year 2000. The Lockheed TriStar and McDonnell-Douglas DC-10, too, have many years ahead of them. Europe's Airbus also appears to be sufficiently well-established to hold its own against American competition. Improved engines and new materials will result in better versions of these aircraft but they will remain unchallenged except for a few completely new designs.

Experimental transports built for military purposes may indicate the path that could be taken by some civil designs. The Boeing YC-14 and the McDonnell-Douglas YC-15 aircraft were designed for the AMST (advanced medium short take-off and landing) competition in the United States. About the size of a Boeing 727, these aircraft can carry passengers and cargo into short airstrips but lack of funds interrupted their development. The Boeing design used the Coanda effect to produce the high lift necessary for STOL flying. Named after a Belgian aviation pioneer, the Coanda effect exploits the tendency of air to follow a curved surface. By placing the jet engines above the wing, Boeing's designers could pro-duce a powerful 'flap' of air to enable the aircraft to fly slowly (figure 1). The McDonnell-Douglas entry for the AMST competition achieved a STOL performance by placing a 'venetian blind' of flaps behind the exhaust from the engines, directing the thrust downward. Either or both of these aircraft seem certain to appear as airliners or as military transports.

The Boeing 747 seems destined to hold its place as the world's largest passenger airliner, for 600-seat versions are required by several airlines and yet a further increase in the size of the fuselage could bring the capacity to nearly 1,000. A German industrial designer has produced several models designed to provoke fresh thinking on aircraft design.

Aircraft such as the McDonnel-Douglas YC-15 (*below*) could point the way to STOL (Short Take-Off and Landing) services by large airliners.

This vertical take-off airliner (*above*) was proposed some years ago by Hawker-Siddeley but was never built.

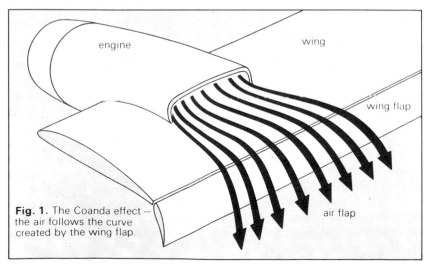

Fig. 1. The Coanda effect — the air follows the curve created by the wing flap.

engine

wing

wing flap

air flap

Impressed by the efficient shape of the shark – a streamlined design which has been around for a million years or so – Luigi Colani modelled one of his ideas to look remarkably like this terror of the deep.

Slightly less fanciful ideas are being studied by Boeing and McDonnell-Douglas, who foresee giant strides in the air cargo business; to date almost all cargo aircraft were designed originally as passenger airliners and have subsequently been modified to carry freight. One strange shape being studied by Boeing features a tandem wing configuration – a layout which has the benefit of providing the required area without resulting in a high wing span. Other more conventional shapes also being studied feature a wide fuselage capable of accommodating many containers. Boeing foresee a 'family' of such freighters, sized to operate over routes of varying densities.

Not to be outdone, McDonnell-Douglas too are studying various freighter layouts, including a wide-fuselage 'Nation Builder' with a payload of more than 340,000 pounds – that's about the weight of an empty Boeing 747! As early as 1910, Professor Hugo Junkers conceived the notion of a trans-Atlantic airliner capable of carrying all its passengers in the wing. In the G.38 Junkers tested his concept, some of its 34 passengers being carried in the wing, but although several

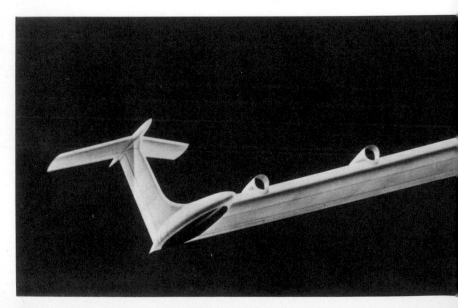

designers have produced flying-wings, none has been a commercial success. Both Boeing and McDonnell-Douglas are looking afresh at the flying wing with a view to producing giant freighters. Loaded through doors at the wing tips, these aircraft would be capable of carrying many containers and bulky cargo. The first of these flying wings would weigh about one million pounds but Boeing envisage a later nuclear-powered design capable of carrying 1,700 passengers and 660,000 pounds of freight at 960 km/h (600 mph) over an unlimited range.

If the airship protagonists have their way, aeroplanes will not be the only means of air transport in the future. Advances in materials and engines are encouraging designers to consider the re-introduction of this quiet and graceful form of transport.

The growing fuel costs have led several designers to blow the dust off airship projects and some are now being built. Most are intended to carry cargo, having a considerable advantage over aircraft in that they can hover over a factory to pick up heavy loads. The Thermo-Skyship planned as both a cargo and passenger carrier features a giant airfoil shape and jet engine propulsion. Several nations are working on airship projects and there does seem to be a future for this type of aircraft.

This giant flying wing is one futuristic design being proposed for air freight tasks.

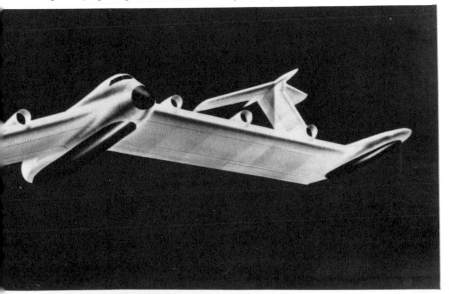

Other forms of communication in the twenty-first century are likely to make a considerable impact on air transport. Lasers, satellites and television screens will play a growing part in communications, reducing the need for businessmen to fly around the world to attend meetings. The advances in electronics which will reduce the need for business travel will also improve the productivity of factories so that people will have more leisure time – and that means more holidays too. So the percentage of holidaymakers travelling on the jumbos of tomorrow is likely to go on increasing, boosting tourism in many parts of the world.

Although most of the airliners of the future are likely to be high-capacity aircraft designed to fly large numbers of passengers at low cost, high-speed airliners will also have a place in the scheme of things. The Concorde has 'only' to cope with temperatures of up to 150°C: the second-generation supersonic transports will carry larger numbers of passengers and will somehow have to withstand some 280°C. But that, of course, is only the beginning! The Space-Shuttle Orbiter built by Rockwell for NASA's space programme points the way to passenger travel in the next century. Later, hypersonic airliners capable of speeds of 6,400 km/h (4,000 mph) will speed 500 passengers to the edge of the atmosphere, bouncing on their way across the top of the

atmosphere until they re-enter and land at their destinations.

Some advances in aviation will be less revolutionary in terms of speed but no less important in their effect upon our civilisation. Experiments are taking place which could lead to the production of large 'ground effect' aircraft. These strange-looking craft skim over the surface within ground-effect (on a bubble of air, you might say). Unlike hovercraft, however, these craft can fly like a normal aeroplane, hopping over obstacles before returning to low level and a ground-effect bubble. These craft are very

The shape of travel to come — the Space Shuttle will be rocketed into space, and return to land like an aeroplane.

economical, expending little energy on keeping aloft on the air bubble created by the wing shape.

Just as the shapes of airliners will change, so, too, smaller light aircraft will be very different from the Piper Cherokees and Cessna Skyhawks of today. Piston engines will probably continue in use for the next decade or so but aircraft such as the Rutan Varieze and the VFW Fanliner could well be the shapes of things to come. Changes inside aircraft will be no less dramatic in the coming years. Cathode ray tube instrument panels are likely to become commonplace, replacing the many different dials and lights on present-day flight decks. As computers take over the control of aircraft a single handle will probably replace the control column and rudder bars of today. In the passenger cabin television screens may replace the larger screens used for showing films on present-day aircraft. As well as showing films, they may receive television programmes from communications satellites. Safety instructions could also be given on the screens. In the first class cabins of some airliners today, telephones are available for communication with the ground – by radio link. Perhaps it will be possible in future to improve this facility by allowing the passengers to see their partner on a screen.

Whatever the future brings, you may be sure that aviation will play its part with faster and larger airliners.

211

Airlines of the World

Facts correct at time of going to press.

Aer Lingus (Ireland)
Founded 1936
Fleet ~~🛫 ▬▬~~ 21
Employees 6,010

Aeroflot (U.S.S.R.)
Founded 1923
Fleet ~~2500~~ + ~~▬▬~~ 2500
Employees 500,000

Air Canada (Canada)
Founded as Trans-Canada
Air Lines 1937
126 Fleet ~~🛫 ▬▬~~
Employees 20,964

Air France (France)
Founded 1933
105 Fleet ~~🛫 ▬▬~~
Employees 32,389

Air India (India)
Founded as Air-India
International 1946
Fleet ~~🛫 ▬▬~~ 14
Employees 12,676

Air Jamaica (Jamaica)
Founded 1968
Fleet 10
Employees 1,205

Air New Zeland (New Zealand)
Founded as Tasman Empire
Airways 1939
Fleet ~~🛫 ▬~~ 35
Employees 8,900
180

Alia – Royal Jordanian Airlines (Jordan)
Founded 1963
Fleet 9
Employees 2,116

Alitalia (Italy)
Founded 1946
62 Fleet ~~🛫 ▬▬~~
Employees 17,040

American Airlines (USA)
Founded 1934
Fleet ~~🛫 ▬▬~~ 232
Employees 38,000

All Nippon Airways (Japan)
Founded 1952
Fleet ~~🛫 ▬▬~~ 96
Employees 9,854

Austrian Airlines (Austria)
Founded 1958
Fleet ~~🛫 ▬▬~~ 14
Employees 2,057

Braniff International Airways (USA)
Founded as Braniff Airways 1930
Fleet ~~🛫 ▬▬~~ 107
Employees 13,500

British Airways (United Kingdom)
Founded 1972 by merger of BEA and BOAC
Fleet ~~🛫 ▬▬~~
Employees 53,900

British Caledonian
Airways (United Kingdom)
Founded 1970
Fleet 29
Employees 6,100

Dan-Air Services (United
Kingdom)
Founded 1953
Fleet 48
Employees 3,500

British Midland Airways
(United Kingdom)
Founded 1938
Fleet 13
Employees 1,059

Delta Air Lines (USA)
Founded as passenger
airline 1929
Fleet 204
Employees 35,000

Cathay Pacific Airways
(Hong Kong)
Founded 1946
Fleet 16
Employees 4,137

Eastern Air Lines (USA)
Founded 1938
Fleet 250
Employees 37,000

China Airlines (Taiwan)
Founded 1959
Fleet 18
Employees 4,246

Egyptair (Egypt)
Founded as Misr Airwork
1931
Fleet 18
Employees 9,610

Condor Flugdienst
(Germany)
Founded by Lufthansa in
1961
Fleet 17
Employees 1,100

El Al (Israel)
Founded 1948
Fleet 16
Employees 5,652

CAAC (Civil Aviation
Administration of China)
Founded 1949
Fleet 50

The Flying Tiger Line
(USA)
Founded as National Skyway
Freight 1945
Fleet 28
Employees 4,761

CSA (Ceskoslovenskě
Aerolinie) Czechoslovakia
Founded 1923
Fleet 57
Employees 6,006

Cyprus Airways (Cyprus)
Founded 1947
Fleet 11
Employees 685

Gulf Air
Founded 1950
Fleet 27
Employees 3,500

Indian Airlines (India)
Founded 1953
Fleet ~~45~~ 45
Employees 15,117

Lufthansa (Germany)
Founded (original company)
1926
Fleet ~~95~~ 95
Employees 29,400

Iran Air (Iran)
Founded 1962
Fleet ~~21~~ 21

Iraqi Airways (Iraq)
Founded 1945
Fleet 18
Employees 4,000

MEA — Middle East Airlines Airliban (Lebanon)
Founded 1945
Fleet 21
Employees 4,778

Japan Air Lines (Japan)
Founded 1951
Fleet 83
Employees 20,600

Mount Cook Airlines (New Zealand)
Founded 1920
Fleet 31
Employees 160

JAT — Jugoslovenski Aerotransport (Yugoslavia)
Founded 1947
Fleet 29
Employees 5,663

Nigeria Airways (Nigeria)
Founded 1958
Fleet 22
Employees 4,493

KLM Royal Dutch Airlines (Netherlands)
Founded 1919
56 Fleet
Employees 17,800

Northwest Orient Airlines (USA)
Founded as US air mail company in 1926
Fleet 106
Employees 10,680

Laker Airways (United Kingdom)
Founded 1966
Fleet ~~130~~ 30
Employees ~~1,071~~ 0
Went Bust 1982!

Olympic Airways (Greece)
42 Founded 1957
Fleet ~~~~
Employees 8,974

Libyan Arab Airlines (Libya)
Founded as Kingdom of Libya Airlines 1964
Fleet 21
Employees 2,500

Pakistan International Airlines — PIA (Pakistan)
Founded 1955
Fleet 27
Employees 19,469

Pan American World
Airways (USA)
Founded 1927
Fleet 82
Employees 26,678

Qantas (Australia)
Founded 1920
23 Fleet ▮▮▮▮
Employees 13,174

Royal Iberia (Spain)
Founded 1927
94 Fleet ▮▮
Employees 23,116

Sabena (Belgium)
Founded 1923
Fleet ▮▮▮▮ 39
Employees 9,848

SAS — Scandinavian
Airlines System (Denmark,
Norway, & Sweden)
Founded 1946
68 Fleet ▮
Employees 16,010

SAS

Saudia — Saudi Arabian
Airlines (Saudi Arabia)
Founded 1945
Fleet 60
Employees 11,250

Seabord World Airlines
(USA)
Founded 1947
Fleet 13
Employees 1,700

Singapore Airlines
(Singapore)
Founded 1972
Fleet 36
Employees 7,900

South African Airways
(South Africa)
Founded 1934
Fleet 41
Employees 10,387

Swissair (Switzerland)
Founded 1931
Fleet ▮ 51
Employees 14,692

TAP Air Portugal
Founded 1944
Fleet 26
Employees 8,949

Trans World Airlines —
TWA (USA)
Founded 1926
198 Fleet ▮▮
Employees 35,897

TWA

United Airlines (USA)
Founded 1931
Fleet 363
Employees 54,264

UTA — Union de
Transports Aeriens
(France)
Founded 1963
Fleet 17
Employees 6,882

Varig (Brazil)
Founded 1927
Fleet ▮▮▮▮ 39
Employees 15,568

The Development of Flight

Percy Pilcher with an early hang-glider.

As long as 200 years ago this balloon crossed the English Channel, carrying the pioneers Blanchard and Jeffries.

1783 The Montgolfier brothers designed and flew the first man-carrying balloon: François Pilâtre de Rozier ascended to a height of 26 metres.

1804 George Cayley designed and built the first model glider, which he developed to carry a man.

1894 Lawrence Hargrave built and flew the first man-carrying kite.

1903 Orville and Wilbur Wright achieved the first-ever powered, man-carrying flight in a heavier-than-air craft, their *Flyer*.

1906 Alberto Santos-Dumont achieved Europe's first powered, man-carrying aeroplane flight.

1909 The first man to cross the English Channel in an aeroplane – Louis Bleriot, in a type XI monoplane.

1914 The first scheduled passenger service was started, by the Benoist Company, between St Petersburg and Tampa in Florida, U.S.A.

1919 The first trans-Atlantic air crossing was achieved by Lieutenant Commander A. C. Read of the U.S. Navy

1919 First non-stop crossing of the Atlantic by Captain John Alcock and Lieutenant Arthur Whitten-Brown in a Vickers Vimy.

1919 First flight from England to Australia completed by Keith and Ross Smith, and two other crew members.

The Cierva autogiro.

1923 First successful flight of a rotating-wing aircraft — Juan de la Cierva's *Autogiro*.

1924 First successful round-the-world flight, by pilots of the U.S. Army air service. Two of the four aircraft crashed en route, the others completed the flight in 175 days.

1926 First aeroplane flight over the North Pole, by Richard Byrd and Floyd Bennett.

1927 First non-stop solo crossing of the Atlantic, by Charles Lindbergh in *Spirit of St Louis*.

1928 First solo flight from Britain to Australia, by Squadron Leader H. J. L. ('Bert') Hinkler.

1928 First trans-Pacific flight, San Francisco to Brisbane, by Charles Kingsford Smith and his crew in *Southern Cross*.

1930 Amy Johnson became first woman to fly solo from England to Australia.

1932 Amelia Earhart became the first woman to fly solo across the Atlantic.

1937 The world's first turbo-jet aircraft engine, deisgned by Frank Whittle, ran for the first time.

1939 The first flight of a turbo-jet powered aircraft, the Heinkel He 178.

1947 Charles Yeager of the United States Air Force flew faster than the speed of sound in a Bell XS-1 rocket-powered aircraft.

1950 The first scheduled passenger service by a helicopter was operated by BEA between Cardiff and Liverpool.

1969 The first flight of the Boeing 747, the first wide-bodied, turbo-jet powered airliner.

1969 The Hawker-Siddley Harrier, the first Vertical/Short Take-off and Land Aircraft, entered service with the R.A.F.

1976 First regular supersonic passenger services inaugurated by British Airways (London—Bahrain) and Air France (Paris—Rio de Janeiro).

The Boeing 747 'jumbo' jet has helped introduce the era of large scale travel at low air fares. Future developments would increase the seating capacity to above 1,000 people.

Airline 2-letter codes

AA	American Airlines	**LZ**	Balkan
AC	Air Canada	**MA**	Malev
AF	Air France	**ME**	Middle East Airlines
AH	Air Algerie	**MH**	Malaysian Airline System
AR	Aerolineas Argentinas	**MS**	Egyptair
AT	Royal Air Maroc	**NW**	Northwest Orient Airlines
AY	Finnair	**OA**	Olympic Airways
AZ	Alitalia	**OK**	CSA
BA	British Airways	**OS**	Austrian Airlines
BN	Braniff International Airways	**PA**	Pan American Airways
BR	British Caledonian Airways	**PK**	Pakistan International Airlines
CA	General Administration of Civil Aviation of China	**PR**	Philippine Airlines
		QC	Air Zaire
CP	CP Air	**QF**	Qantas Airways
DL	Delta Air Lines	**QZ**	Zambia Airways
EA	Eastern Air Lines	**RG**	Varig
EI	Aer Lingus	**RJ**	Alia The Royal Jordanian Airlines
ET	Ethiopian Airlines		
FG	Ariana Afghan Airlines	**RK**	Air Afrique
FI	Icelandair	**RO**	Tarom
GA	Garuda Indonesian Airways	**SA**	South African Airways
GF	Gulf Air	**SK**	Scandinavian Airlines
GH	Ghana Airways	**SN**	Sabena
HA	Hawaiian Airlines	**SQ**	Singapore Airlines
IA	Iraqi Airways	**SR**	Swissair
IB	Iberia	**SU**	Aeroflot Soviet Airlines
IR	Iran National Airlines	**SV**	Saudia
JL	Japan Air Lines	**TE**	Air New Zealand
JU	Jugoslovenski Aerotransport	**TG**	Thai Airways International
KL	KLM Royal Dutch Airlines	**TP**	TAP Air Portugal
KM	Air Malta	**TU**	Tunis Air
KQ	Kenya Airways	**TW**	Trans World Airlines
KU	Kuwait Airways	**UA**	United Airlines
LH	Lufthansa	**UT**	UTA
LO	LOT Polish Airlines	**VA**	VIASA
LY	El Al Israel Airlines	**WT**	Nigerian Airways

IATA 3-Letter Codes

This is but a random selection from hundreds of towns and cities. Try to learn the codes; airline staff will know these codes as well as dozens more:

ABZ	Aberdeen
AGP	Malaga
AMS	Amsterdam
ATH	Athens
BEY	Beirut
BFS	Belfast
BHX	Birmingham
BKK	Bangkok
BRU	Brussels
BUE	Buenos Aires
CAI	Cairo
CDG	Paris Charles de Gaulle
CGN	Cologne
CPH	Copenhagen
CPT	Cape Town
DAR	Dar-es-Salaam
DME	Moscow Domodedovo
DUB	Dublin
EDI	Edinburgh
EZE	Buenos Aires-Ezeiza
FCO	Rome Fiumicino
FRA	Frankfurt
GCI	Guernsey
GLA	Glasgow Abbotsinch
GOA	Genoa
HAJ	Hanover
HEL	Helsinki
HKG	Hong Kong Kai Tak
IAD	Washington Dulles

IBZ	Ibiza
IST	Istanbul
JFK	New York J. F. Kennedy
LAX	Los Angeles International
LGW	London Gatwick
LHR	London Heathrow
LIS	Lisbon
LTN	Luton
MAD	Madrid Barajas
MAN	Manchester
MEL	Melbourne
MIL	Milan
NBO	Nairobi International
NCL	Newcastle
ORY	Paris Orly
PEK	Peking
PMI	Palma Mallorca
RHO	Rhodes
RIO	Rio de Janeiro
SFO	San Francisco International
SVO	Moscow Shevemetyevo
SZG	Salzburg
TLV	Tel Aviv Ben Gurion
TUN	Tunis
ULN	Ulan Bator
VCE	Venice
VCP	Sao Paulo Viracopos
VIE	Vienna
WAW	Warsaw ·
WLG	Wellington
WTS	Tsiroanomandidy
XPK	Pukatawagan (Canada)
YQB	Quebec City
YUL	Montreal Dorval
YYZ	Toronto-International
ZRH	Zurich

Useful Addresses

For British Airways sponsorship for pilot training, contact:
College of Air Training,
Selection Department,
Hamble,
Southampton SO3 5NA

Details of the airline's Engineering Apprenticeship and Graduate Training schemes may be obtained from:
British Airways,
Recruitment and Selection Services,
Comet House,
Building 48,
London Heathrow Airport,
Hounslow,
Middlesex.

Another body which does much to promote an interest in aviation is
The Air League,
4 Hamilton Place,
London W1V 0BQ.
As well as providing information on the aircraft industry, the Air League does award scholarships for training.

Opportunities for employment in the airline and travel industries are rather limited and there are always more applicants than vacancies. For the really determined, advice may be obtained from:
The Air Transport and Travel
    Industry Training Board,
Staines House,
High Street,
Staines,
Middlesex TW18 4AS.
As the title suggests, the Board is primarily concerned with helping companies to train their staff but it can provide information on apprentice and other schemes.

For those who have no desire to make a career in aviation but are nevertheless interested in the subject, membership of a society for enthusiasts could be very rewarding.
Air Britain, the International Association of Aviation Historians,
208 Stock Road,
Billericay,
Essex CM12 0SH.
This group publishes a magazine and many booklets of interest to the aviation enthusiast.

The World's Top Ten Airports

Advice on the educational requirements for the travel industry may be obtained from:
The Institute of Travel and
    Tourism,
53/54 Newman Street,
London W1P 4JJ
A number of Colleges and Institutes of Higher Education in the U.K. offer the Institute courses. Correspondence courses are also run by the Institute.

Useful skills for a career in aviation can be learned in the Royal Air Force. Youngsters must be prepared to devote several years to the Service and indeed many will find it an interesting and absorbing life. Many large towns have Careers Information offices but details of air and ground jobs may be obtained from
The Office Commander,
Careers Information Office,
Kelvin House,
Cleveland Street,
London W.1.
University graduate and apprentice schemes are available.

This listing is in terms of international traffic. A number of American airports are used by more passengers but the majority are on domestic flights.

London (Heathrow)
New York (J. F. Kennedy)
Frankfurt
Washington (Dulles)
Amsterdam
Paris (Charles de Gaulle)
Paris (Orly)
Copenhagen
Rome
London (Gatwick)

John F. Kennedy Airport — America's most important gateway.

Index